T0107482

LEGS OF IRON

*Revealing life sketches of
Pauline Wiltshire*

Pauline Wiltshire and
Albert A C Waite

iUniverse, Inc.
Bloomington

LEGS OF IRON
Revealing life sketches of Pauline Wiltshire

iUniverse books may be ordered through booksellers or by contacting:

iUniverse
1663 Liberty Drive
Bloomington, IN 47403
www.iuniverse.com
1-800-Authors (1-800-288-4677)

Because of the dynamic nature of the Internet, any web addresses or links contained in this book may have changed since publication and may no longer be valid.

ISBN: 978-1-4620-0788-2 (sc)
ISBN: 978-1-4620-0732-5 (ebk)

Printed in the United States of America

iUniverse rev. date: 4/22/2011

This book is lovingly dedicated to the memories of Charlotte (Mama), Aunt Ina and all those who do similar good

COMMENTS

Pauline's character comes over strongly and she has led such an interesting life!

It is a good idea to introduce the details of her disabilities towards the middle of the book so that we see her as a person first and a disabled person much later when we have got to 'know' her.

I could almost wish that the book was twice as long.

EB (*A Librarian*)

This looks good. Congratulations and well done!

RD (*A PR Consultant*)

Contents

ACKNOWLEDGEMENTS

There are a number of well meaning individuals who have encouraged and cautiously nudged for this book to be written. You know who you are. Your positive and encouraging comments and vision are acknowledged.

Three ladies, however, must be singled out:

Alicia A. C. Waite, RM and DM for reading the material at different times. Their suggestions, where accepted, have enhanced the work.

The Authors, however, accept full responsibility for the accuracy and presentation of this work.

From the Bio-Author

Up to the time of writing this page I have not met Pauline Wiltshire, the co-author of this book. However, through numerous telephone conversations I have met a personality that exudes energy, transmits her dreams, exposed her strengths and a little weakness with steel-like determination. And it has caused me to re-evaluate my understanding of the well known quote, "The mind is the measure of the [person]."

It was around September 2004 that my home telephone rang. On the other end the person said, "My name is Pauline. Dr Richard DeLisser said you could help me to publish my book." The outcome of that initial and two other lengthy telephone conversations was that I decided to interview Pauline and put her story to paper.

Pauline wanted the book to be published quickly. I made no promises but thought it could be completed by December 2005. Time is a rare commodity even though each one of us has exactly the same amount – twenty-four hours in the day or 31,536,000 seconds in an ordinary year. It would take me half a working day to travel to

Pauline's home to interview her and that was unthinkable! The economy of time demanded that it would have to be done by telephone interviews.

We agreed on three sessions a week, the days and times. The first session, which was the shortest, lasted for about two hours and was conducted on 1 November 2004. Each time I followed a set of prepared questions to guide the interview. By the end of the first set of interviews in early December that year, I had read letters, scrapbooks and Pauline's book, *Living and Winning*. The outlines I constructed for the interviews worked well. But from then until even now, over three years later, my telephone still would ring periodically, and with a telephone-transmitted smile, Pauline would share snippets of information for me to consider including in the book. The next set of interviews was completed on 25 May 2008.

Clearly, at the time of writing this, it is not 2005. An M4 motorway pile-up I was involved in has impacted my work schedule but provided more reflective time for Pauline to add a few more details here and there. With some of these snippets included, we hope that *Legs of Iron* will impact the mind of the reader in a constructive manner, bringing about the fruition of some of Pauline's dreams.

Some of the names of individuals in the book are changed to make their identities less obvious.

AACW
Conifers
October 2008

Chapter ONE

More Than An Introduction

I am grateful for my two homes: the land of my birth, Jamaica, and my adopted home, London, England. Jamaica provided me with the skills to survive independently, while London provided the opportunity to live out those skills.

Readers will make up their minds as to why and if this book is necessary. I have not made up my mind as to the type of impact it will have on all, for like art, the interpretation of its content, and the appreciation of the life sketches and their usefulness, is in the eyes of the reader. I will therefore concur with and gratefully accept all positive reasons attributed to the impact this book may have achieved, and learn from any constructive observations made.

I would, however, state a few core and deeply felt outcomes I would hope that this book conveys to society as a whole and to individuals in particular. If I am only partly successful in achieving these objectives it will have been well worth the effort.

The book, which is somewhat biographical, is written in an easily readable style, but the punch, I hope, will be heavyweight.

At this stage I have chosen not to detail the extent of my disability. This is for no other reason than to allow the reader to focus on key aspects of my story, without the distraction of the nature and details of my disability. However, those who see it as a vantage point to be familiar with the intricacies of my disability, *you* can fast forward to chapter ten where the specifics are laid out. For the rest of you, it is sufficient to say, to coin a phrase, that I am a *multiple-physically* disabled woman.

The main purpose of this book is to inform, inspire and raise the awareness of society – both able-bodied and not so able-bodied - of the fertile mind and feelings of a disabled person. In doing so, it is hoped that:

Parents of disabled children will better understand how to relate to and treat their offspring; the general public will get a glimpse of a disabled person's mind, hopes, ambitions and feelings; people will learn not to judge a person only by his or her appearance but to understand that the mind is more so the measure of the person - so that society will reduce the pressure (which induces a sense of guilt and shame for having 'one of them') they put on parents with disabled children. This often results in parents restricting their child's public appearances, treating them as lesser humans or even locking them away when visitors come to the home, in an attempt to deny their existence, which in effect dehumanises their own children.

Another reason for this book is to inform the various departments in local government, particularly Social Services, Health and Housing, that all I ever needed was to be helped to live a *normal life*; to have my own things and to recognise that I am simply differently abled; to live with self-respect, values, ambition and a zest for the quality of life that I am comfortable with.

I hope just to let society know or even to start to understand that I don't want them to apologise for my disability or look away embarrassed when I am around. I am who I am and will be the best I can be for as long as life permits. No pity. No bad treatment. No dehumanising. Is that too much to expect from an intelligent and civilised western society?

Finally, it is my dream that this book will go some way to help my son to ignore society's pressures and norms and start to feel comfortable with just being my son. This is a tall order for him - it is difficult to be *an island* in a society that makes it almost impossible for him to be proud of his disabled mother.

I don't blame my son for his indifference towards me. My mother also succumbs to society's norms. I was the *not seen* daughter. In fact I was an adult before I knew who my real mother was. Society must carry its share of the blame for this.

***

I am grateful for my two homes: the land of my birth, Jamaica, and my adopted home, London, England. Jamaica provided me with the skills to survive independently, while London provided the opportunity to live out those skills.

Before the age of 13, I was equipped with skills that many18 year-olds in England could only dream of. The challenges and hardships of my Jamaican country-life forced me to learn to wash with my hands, clean floors on my knees, cook food on open wooden fires and walk for miles.

England provided its challenges and hardships too - different types but just as demanding. However, I was equipped to meet and transform them into opportunities. Additional luxuries like a regular bus service, a washing machine, a vacuum cleaner and eventually my own accommodation, have made 'normal' living easier and life more comfortable.

My early childhood was hard, but I didn't realize it until I was aged four and a half. Earlier, I was emotionally stable but ill-equipped to cope physically. I thought I was a single-parent child – no father. Later I was to discover the stark reality of what I had thought – right on both counts, but not in a way of which I could have dreamt. Eventually, and under secretive circumstances, I discovered who one of my real parents was. A stranger with whom I had no emotional attachment, turned out to be my real mother.

As a child I was ignored and even treated unkindly by a stranger who came to live for a short time in my home. She turned out to be my real mother. But during those times, even though I was denied my real mother's love, I was not denied a mother's love! Providence had it that the 'stranger within our gates' was my biological mother, who compensated for the bad start I had had in life, by sending for me, her severely handicapped child, to join her in the motherland, England. She didn't have to, but she did and I am eternally grateful to her. I love my real mother for availing me of the opportunities in my adopted home, London.

I have said (in *Living and Winning*) and may still say some uncomfortable truths about my mother, but this is merely in the interest of openness and for the world to see how society places pressure on parents of handicapped children, forcing them to conform to its charter and compass of normality.

My limited early education and physical disability further deprived me of the skills and expressiveness to be normal in society's eyes. Still, I have a creative mind atop what I term a *multiple-physically-handicapped* body. I can see and I can walk. I can talk - maybe, not to society's chartered normality, but my comprehension is 'normal' and my thinking is 'normal' too. I have learnt much from listening. I understand much more than I am expected to. I have good advice to give. But is anyone prepared to listen?

This book is a reflection of life in my two homes: Jamaica and England.

Chapter TWO

I'm Disabled -
I'm Not A Fool

I was given the smallest glass of drink, even though I am the eldest and certainly not the smallest. I would laugh inside to myself, 'Do they think I can't see? Or do they think I lack understanding?

From time to time, people from different education backgrounds seek my advice on social and interpersonal issues. My hard-knock experiences, and having given birth to a normal child, have given me some skills to assess social problems objectively and suggest solutions. This ability has been with me ever since I lived in Jamaica, and was probably first identified in its infancy, when I was in the Kingston Public Hospital (KPH) for procedures on my leg.

In 2004 my adopted father, Phillip, at the age of 82 planned to get married in Florida, where he lives. It was only a year after my aunt, his wife, had died. We discussed my attendance at the wedding and he expressed his desire to see me present. Unfortunately, because of a hospital appointment I could not go, but I was satisfied that I was valued enough for my presence to be welcomed. There are closer family members to whom he could have allocated my place and ignored me without causing anyone hurt. However, I was considered to be significant enough to be included in the family list.

I was made aware that my adopted father wanted to take me to live in America long before I came to England, some 30 years ago. But I was always told the reason he could not was because I was *adopted.* (My adoption was not official. In Jamaica a more well-to-do family member could take a child into their home and look after them as a member of that family. Apart from the consent of the two families, no papers were necessary.) I never accepted that as a valid reason and felt it was more to do with my disability. Uncle Sam didn't want the burden of a severely disabled person in his country, the land of the brave and free. I was not perceived as being capable of doing much physical work and America needed a labour-force. This, as the reader will see later, was not quite accurate.

***

During the process of co-authoring this book I was encouraged to look more closely at my birth certificate. This is what it reveals:

Birth in the district of: Coleyville
Parish of: Manchester
Date of Birth: sixteenth January 1950

Place of Birth: Mason Run

Sex: Female

Name of Father:

Name, Surname and Maiden name of Mother: Doris Wiltshire, a domestic, 25 years

Profession of Father:

Signature, Qualification and Residence of Informant: Charlotte Hewitt, Cousin present at birth. Mason Run, Manchester

When Registered: Fourteenth February 1950.

The obvious omission is information about a father. But while it would have been good to see those slots filled in, I know that it is not unusual for a father's details to be absent on a child's birth certificate. I know also that that is not a particular feature of the 1950s or before, or since, of the Jamaican society, even given the popularisation in songs, documentaries and theatre productions of the *absence of baby fathers* in that country. Even here in Britain, there are many who do not have the comfort of looking at their birth certificates and seeing information about their father filled in. So much so that Britain is now making it a necessity for a father's name to be included in every child's birth details. The problem, it seems to me, is not because fathers are particularly unaccountable, but rather, society and human nature are such that if it were the man who was to carry the baby, it would be the mother's details that would be missing. That's the way life is. If it is convenient people will get away with whatever they can.

There, however, seems to be complete silence as to why it is my Aunt Doris, listed as aged 25, that is recorded on my birth certificate as my mother. I now know that in

1950, Aunt Doris, who was born about 1910 was closer 40 years old than 25. But my cousin Charlotte Hewitt, who registered me and was present at my birth, would not have known Aunt Doris's age. What did it matter? She was not my real mother and although no harm was intended, the objective was to give the correct details of the date and place of my birth. That, Charlotte did achieve.

But why was Aunt Doris named as my mother when I didn't even live with her for a day? She was in fact living in Connecticut, USA, at the time of my birth and had been there for some time. Was it that my disability, discovered at birth, gave my real mother a shock and therefore I was rejected? Or was it something to do with the rumoured secrets surrounding the man who actually fathered me that caused my absentee Aunt Doris, who did not have any children of her own, to be identified, before my birth, to be named as my mother? To complicate the matter further, I'm only one year and seven months older than my mother's next child. What does this suggest? Hmmm!

Yet another set of unanswered questions: Why was Charlotte present at my birth? Was she to be my guardian until I could be sent to Aunt Doris in the USA, who would then 'grow' me up as her own child in the then Jamaican tradition? Was this the reason her name was on my birth certificate as my mother, and Charlotte's was recorded as being present at my birth, because she was? Was there a non-negotiable agreement struck-up before my birth to list Aunt Doris as my mother and therefore, even though I 'came out' disabled her name had to go down in the mother's slot on the certificate? Clearly, unlike the father's, the mother's slots on the certificate form had to be filled in at the hospital at the time of birth. Was my real mother, therefore, registered in the hospital in the name of Aunt Doris? Did I end up with Charlotte because, when it was discovered that I was disabled, Aunt Doris became the second person to reject me? Or, was that the plan for me to stay with Charlotte until it was convenient for Aunt Doris to come to Jamaica and take me with her back to Connecticut?

Charlotte treated me like a normal child and loved me like any loving mother would. Why? Was it because Charlotte knew real pain as a mother? By the time I was born Charlotte had had the sad misfortune of burying her only child, a daughter, and her child – Charlotte's granddaughter. Was I the fortunate beneficiary of the innate love my cousin, Charlotte - a mother and grandmother - had overflowing with no one to give it to? Was that the reason I was cared for by 'mama' with such affection and dedication?

I still do not have answers to these and a host of other questions. It would be easy to say that it was because I was severely disabled that I acquired an apparently absentee adopted mother while a cousin cared for me, as a mother, and that that was thought to be the best outcome for every one. But even that simplistic conclusion would be a guess. My disability, however, has defined who I am and who society thinks I am and how I should be treated. That is not a guess.

***

In 1999 I went on holiday with my sisters and cousins from London to the United States. I noticed that both at my mum's place and when we visited other family members, including Aunt Doris and Phillip's home, I was given the smallest glass of drink, even though I am the eldest and certainly not the smallest. I would laugh inside to myself, 'Do they think I can't see? Or do they think I lack understanding? How could they? With the experience that they have had with me, could they be thinking that my brain is handicapped too?' I pitied them, but drank the drinks and sometimes asked for more! Those who have been around me over the years should acknowledge my ability to analyse a situation and think out a coping strategy. I was often angry but kept it deep inside. The pain of being ignored and even ill-treated was real and quite likely visible at times.

In March 2008, five years after Aunt Doris had died, I was having a telephone conversation with Phillip. I just imagined him lounging in his Florida pad with his relatively new wife. I had been reflecting: When Aunt Doris was alive she had declared her love for me, albeit at a safe distance away. While in Jamaica as a little child I had a few items of clothes that Charlotte said came from her. On one of her visits to Jamaica, when I was 14, Aunt Doris did tell me she was my aunt but I don't remember her giving me anything on that visit. I had and have nothing to show that I could definitely say I received directly from her hand.

There was, however, my white dolly, which I named Betty, which Charlotte told me had come from Aunt Doris. Betty would cry when I squeezed her tummy and would close her eyes when I lay her on her back. I had endless hours of joy playing with Betty. I didn't mind other children, who often stayed with Charlotte, playing with Betty, so as long as they took good care of her. One day it had just started to rain when I heard Charlotte shouted, "What's Celia doing in the rain with that backra (of white European decent) pickney?" I rushed to the front door and was just in time to meet a running Celia on the steps who pushed Betty into my outstretched arms. I wiped the drops of rain from Betty's face, legs and arms and placed her to sleep in her special corner on the floor. She was safe and with that assurance I could get on with my other activities.

In my reflections though, I reasoned, 'Aunt Ina died and I was not left anything.' That was understandable as she had three sons and grandchildren to inherit her estate. One could also reason that I had my fair share whilst I was living with her. I became a little troubled, however, when I thought of Aunt Doris' situation. Her name was listed on my birth certificate as my mother. She had no children of her own even though she had fostered some. Both Phillip and Aunt Doris had said they loved me. So I decided to checkout the love thing.

At a convenient point in the telephone conversation I said, "Dad, how come I'm supposed to be the adopted daughter and Aunt Doris died and I got nothing?"

"If there was a will, that has been destroyed long before I came down here from Connecticut," he said dismissively. As far as I know Phillip has no biological children and his new wife has one child that is married. I don't know if there are any strong connections with any of the children Aunt Doris and Phillip fostered. But there was no indication during that conversation that could make me believe that I would eventually inherit anything from him. As we spoke he became more and more uninterested. Then he said it,

"Time fi dem tings leave me now." (Meaning: It is time I stop worrying about things like that.) It was clear that I would not be receiving any 'dead-left'. But there is one thing about Phillip that is satisfying: He never treated me as if I had no brain.

***

Over the years I have dealt with several local government departments, in order to secure my basic rights:

Long before New Labour considered the ill effects of smoking in public, I intervened at my local Tenants' Association to ban smoking in the meetings. I protested that passive smoking was dangerous to all of us, but more so to those who had breathing problems. It was difficult to get everyone to understand the damage they were causing by smoking at the table, but in time our meetings became smokeless events.

Back in 1988, I was accused of trying to defraud the Social Services Benefit Department (SSD) of £150 of Child Benefit money. I knew nothing about this money - I was not getting any child benefits. Naturally, I refused to pay when told to do so. They threatened me with court action, so I paid a visit to the local SSD office in Sylvester Road to argue my case.

On the day of the appointment I was suffering from a cold and to make things worst I had an attack of asthma. I didn't want to cancel the appointment as I was getting fed up with the accusation of stealing. I knew that my ailments would make it difficult for me to be understood, so I took along a good friend of mine from our Tenants' Association to do the usual double job - 'Hey! I'm credible.

I have white friends to speak on my behalf.' It didn't work. The officer refused to let my friend sit in with me. This was unheard of. By dint of sheer determination, I went in alone, reasoning that it was their responsibility to make sense of what I had to say, given my muffled tone at the time.

I told the officer exactly what I thought of their accusation and made it known that I felt they were treating me worse than an animal. The issue was resolved with an apology; they said they were very sorry to have put me through all this unnecessary harassment.

Winning that case was not sweet. A very bitter taste remained in my mouth from the thought that the SSD had been convinced that I was a liar and a cheat. I might be *strong headed*, but I am neither of those.

When my mother heard that I was writing this book, she called me one Sunday from her home in Florida. There was a trace of anxiety in her voice. "Pauline, are you going to write bad things in your next book about me?" Before I could answer she continued, "It isn't nice to disgrace your family in public. Your other book said a lot of bad things about me. I was humiliated."

As she talked and talked, I noticed that mum didn't say that what I wrote was untrue. Was mum learning at last or was she focusing on her feelings and disregarding her disabled daughter's feelings as usual? Maybe she deemed that I was too disabled to have feelings.

My response was instant. "Mum, what you say doesn't matter to me right now. The truth always hurts. You always talk to me as if I am a mentally-retarded three-year-old."

Even though Mum has had a million reasons to stop treating me the way she does, somehow she only remembered that I am no fool when she heard I was about to write more about my past experiences.

I said, "Mum, this book is going to be a lot different from what I wrote before."

"I'm not going to read it." She insisted, stubbornly.

"Don't worry Mum. I'm sure someone else will tell you what's in it."

All my life I have tried to get my family, work colleagues and society in general to recognise that to be physically disabled does not necessarily affect my power to think. Even though those close to me have witnessed my capability to think, analyse and execute well thought out plans, many are somehow unable to see me beyond my physical features. They fail to see that I am only disabled - I am not a fool.

It is partly this lack of seeing me as I am that informs the writing of this book.

Chapter THREE

My Real Mother

"The reason why Miss Hecky won't accept you as a daughter is because you were born out of wedlock," she said trying to sound posh as she stressed the word wedlock.

Up to the age of three I knew no other mother but Charlotte. She did everything for me: loved me, spoke positively and encouragingly to me and played with me like any loving mother would with her own child. I was very content and happy.

It is customary for village people in Jamaica to meet and talk outside in the yard or even on the veranda, depending on how close their relationships are. At the age of three, I remember hearing one lady who was visiting my home ask, "Charlotte, when last did you see her mother?" There was no recognisable response. But from time to time, that same lady or others would make reference to 'her mother.' They weren't talking *to* me, but I soon got the impression that they were talking *about* me.

By the time I was five, I was convinced that there was something mysterious about who my mother was. I had no reason to wish for anyone else other than Charlotte to be my mother. As far as I was concerned, Charlotte was my Mum. That was what I called her. I was happy. But the constant reference to 'her mother' by different people got me curious, though they clearly were not expecting me to understand.

Occasionally a lady who lived about half a mile from my house in Mason Run would pass by. She paid absolutely no attention to me whatsoever and no one ever told me who she was. She was just another passer-by who would exchange pleasantries with the adults in the yard as she walked past our house. Her name was Miss Hecky.

One day I asked the lady who lived next door to us who this Miss Hecky was.

"One day you will find out", she said.

One day indeed, as Miss Hecky's children went by, she pointed discreetly and said, "There's your brother and sister. Miss Hecky is your mother."

"If she is my mother, how comes she isn't living with me?" I responded defiantly.

"One day you will find out," she repeated with a knowing smile.

When I was the age of five, Miss Hecky, her husband and their two children came to live in Charlotte's house with us. No explanation was given for the move. And within a month, Miss Hecky's husband had left for England, promising to send for his wife and children.

Auntie Hecky, as the many children milling around called her, didn't have much to say to me, even though she was living in *my* house. But she was always quick to blame me for the misdeeds of all the other children in the house. It was always my fault, and Auntie Hecky punished me frequently with *licks*. I was the main target for beating. No one would listen to my protests. I was always wrong. Period.

Before I was six, Auntie Hecky took her two children to live with her husband's sister in Kingston, and she went to join her husband in England. I celebrated when they left – one fewer person to hit me or tell me off. I was happy again.

While Auntie Hecky was living with us, the question of who my real mother was often come up. On one such day, Auntie Hecky looked me in the face and said, "Pauline, do you know you were adopted by your Aunt Doris?" Auntie Doris, who was childless, was her bigger sister and by then was living in Connecticut, USA. I didn't respond, for by then, I had a lot more information from the village ladies about who my real mother was supposed to be. Once one of the ladies said, "Shame she won't own you," referring to Auntie Hecky. During all the time she stayed at our house, Auntie Hecky never once hinted that I might be her daughter.

There were a number of rumours, which attempted to explain the secrecy surrounding my real parents. Charlotte wasn't the source of any of them. The woman who told me that Auntie Hecky's two children were my real brother and sister, called me into her house one day and said, while looking to see if anyone was watching, "Pauline, I am going to tell you a secret." There was a mischievous look on her face. "You must promise me not to say a word to anyone - not even Charlotte. Do you promise?"

Her face was getting more serious. It even showed a bit of fear.

"Yes ma'am."

I was all ears. I knew the subject would be about Miss Hecky and was getting a little impatient just waiting for her to take another breath.

"Right," she said, looking again to see if anyone was in the yard. "The reason why Miss Hecky won't accept you as a daughter is because you were born out of wedlock," she said trying to sound posh as she stressed the word *wedlock*. The lady paused, and then looked at my face as if she was expecting me to react. The information so far wasn't anything MI5 would be interested in. She had to dig deeper and come up with something more stark. After all, most of the children in the village were 'born out of wedlock'!

"Yes ma'am." I responded uninterestedly.

"Also, because you are disabled and is 'fool-fool' nobody wants you. She is too proud to admit having a 'fool-fool' *pickney*."

She looked at me inquiringly, but I remained expressionless. I sensed she was building up to something else. I wanted that big secret to come out, so I simply said, "Yes ma'am."

"Some people say Miss Hecky was raped when she got you. And when you were born handicapped, she was too distressed to keep you. So it was poor Charlotte who had mercy on you and took you as her own." She looked at me again, but this time her face said it all: 'There you have it.'

I bowed my head but said nothing. My mind started to churn over and make sense of what I had just heard.

My thoughts were interrupted with the words: "I think the rape thing is a family rumour. I have never heard her mention 'rape'. Maybe your handicap was just a convenient excuse to reject you."

I slowly raised my head and looked the woman in the eyes. Mine were welled up with tears, but not full enough to drop like beads. Instead, my heart must have been bleeding. My only answer was, "Yes ma'am."

As I left, the woman spoke to my back. "Remember now, not a word to anyone."

"Yes ma'am," came the automated response.

Even though the woman who gave me the details about my real mum was a little mischievous, I was relieved that five years of picking up bits and pieces about 'her mum' and the *licks* Auntie Hecky had given me for the things I had not done were at last making sense. I resolved to keep my promise and say 'not a word' and I have not until now, in these pages.

I didn't hear from Auntie Hecky for quite a while. But after two years, my brother and sister joined our real mother in England. I now realise that things were quite difficult for the whole family there. By the time I started to communicate with Miss Hecky on a personal level, I was ten years old and quite a lass. Apparently, she had sent clothes and money for me a few times, but neither Charlotte nor I had received anything. We began to wonder if the girl who was living in Charlotte's house with us had taken everything from the post office and kept them for herself. Not receiving those phantom gifts didn't bother me too much. Nor did I miss not hearing from England.

Chapter FOUR

My First Ten Years In England

They are English; I am disabled and Jamaican. But even if I were not disabled their status as 'English' would normally give them preferential treatment over us, who come to join an established family in the motherland.

I was 26 years old when I found myself at Heathrow airport, London, waiting for someone to take me to my mother's home. I wasn't sure who to expect. I had not been told. Maybe I was too 'fool-fool' to be able to comprehend that kind of information.

My mother spotted me before I saw her. She said, "Come. How are you?" I wasn't expected to give a response. The porter took my luggage to the car. (It was strange seeing a white man doing that kind of work.) I followed behind my mother and stepfather's brother who lived in England. My step-dad was working at the time and couldn't get time off to come and collect me from the airport.

During the journey my mother spoke mostly to the driver. I was never made part of the conversation and I didn't care much. I occupied my time peering through the window at my new surroundings. At one time I saw a tall building and asked, "Mum, what's that building?" That was the first time I addressed my real mother as 'mum'.

"Shut up. You talk too much," came the sharp response.

In my mind I asked myself the question, 'If that is the way she is talking to me now, what's going to happen when we get home?'

"Well Mum, I would like to know where I am."

She didn't answer. I thought to myself again, 'Give her time, she will soon find out who I am. Time will certainly tell.' I was prepared for battle. At 26 I wasn't going to be treated as a 'nobody'.

As soon as we got through the front door my mother said, "This is home." She paused, then said, "I'm going to the shops for about half an hour. If anyone rings the bell, don't open the door." Again, my private thought was, 'Hell, I might be a stranger in a strange land, but I know how to talk to people and open doors.' It wasn't long after she left that the doorbell rang.

"Who is it?" I enquired through the closed door. The person gave his name and asked if he could speak to Mrs Williams.

"Mrs Williams isn't here," I called back. "I am Mrs Williams's daughter." I peeped through the frosty glass in the front door and realised it was somebody I had seen before; so I opened it. It was a man who had lived in my district but had left for England many years earlier.

The man entered the hallway with a surprised, but nervous grin on his face. "What?!" He exclaimed. "When did you come? Miss Hecky didn't tell me you were coming up." He didn't wait for answers and left saying he would return. When mum came I didn't tell her anyone had called. But true to his word, the man came back about an hour after he had left. While they were in the kitchen talking, I went in and said, "Hello Mum." A shocked expression flashed across the man's face. I understood. While we were in Jamaica, the only mother he knew I had was Charlotte. He had left the district while I was a little child, before the rumours about my parents had been circulated.

I spoke to the man in a familiar tone. It was my mother's turn to wear a shocked face. She commented, "You look as if you know each other." There was no response from either of us. When our male visitor left, my mother told me that in future, if anybody came to the house, I should go to my room. I didn't disobey my mother's orders. When visitors were due to come to the house, I would go to my room as soon as I heard the doorbell ring. I would stay in my room for 10 to 15 minutes, and then somehow, I always had a question for my mum.

"Mum, can I have a drink?" "Mum have you seen the comb?" "Mum did you call me?" I was determined that I wasn't going to be kept hidden away. I was going to be an integral part of the family - as my mother's 26-year-old daughter. I knew I had a brain. I intended to play mind gymnastics if I had to. I wasn't going to be treated like a fool.

I knew that it wasn't going to be easy fitting into an established family. Even though my first sister, Daisy, and my brother Daniel shared Charlotte's home in Jamaica with me for a short time, their status then was as visitors, not as family and certainly, to them at the time, not my brother and sister. When they left Jamaica I was ten, Daisy nine and Daniel was five years old. But they had been living in Kingston and I had not seen them for a few years. My two other sisters, Gifty and Gillian were 18 and 16 years olds when I joined the family home in London. They had visited Jamaica two years earlier and knew that I was the older sister.

My first meeting with my two 'English' sisters, when they were on holiday in Jamaica, was pleasant. Gillian, the youngest, took to me from our first encounter. But that was on their holiday, in a strange land, when it was not hard to be courteous for a few weeks of intermittent encounters. It was going to be different now. I was invading their space, sharing their home and was to be known, to their friends, as their sister. Those two were going to be a complex new entity to be discovered, and I knew it. They are English; I am disabled and Jamaican. But even if I were not disabled their status as 'English' would normally give them preferential treatment over us, who come to join an established family in the motherland.

This is a well-understood fact among Caribbean families in Britain, that when older siblings join the family, they virtually become 'second-class' family members. I, being disabled, therefore, could have easily acquired the 'third-class' status. But Daisy and Daniel, who had preceded me by some sixteen years, would have probably broken down some of the barriers by then. In hindsight, and if I were to be realistic, as a disabled sibling invading the home of two sisters who were sixteen and eighteen year olds, it was more likely for me to acquire the 'last-class' category, irrespective of how many rungs my situation removed me from the normal 'second-class'.

Given that Daisy was nine, Daniel five, Gifty three and Gillian only a few months old when the other two Jamaican born siblings came to England, there should have been little or no rivalry existing between them that would be severely harmful to the Jamaican duo. But when I 'invaded', I was 26, Daisy 25, Daniel 21, Gifty 18 and Gillian 16, not a good set of numbers to be living together in one house. And even though I am disabled, I had no intention of being ignored or treated any differently from number one daughter, even though I was a half sister. I didn't know to what extent my brother and sisters were prepared to meet and live with me. Did they know more about the situation surrounding my birth than I knew? Were they made aware of my relationship with Aunt Doris? I doubt it. But to me that didn't matter. I was in England for a better life and that was the base line.

Because of the hard knocks I had had in Jamaica, my defence mechanism was sharpened to meet and deal with any situation I would come into. It was, however, much simpler than I could have hoped for. Yes, there were more than seven heads in the house, but two of them were not my Jamaican born siblings. Both Daisy and Daniel had long since flown the nest and establish their own stable family units: Daisy with three children of her own and Daniel had two. There was no unreasonable tension between my 'English' sisters and me. And Gillian and I got on like a house on fire, and still do.

The house we lived in had six bedrooms, two sitting rooms, two kitchens, one toilet and a separate bathroom with no toilet. Two of the rooms were rented out, one to a couple and the other to a family. I had the smallest room in the house, which was on the third of three floors. My two sisters, who were born in England, and were 16 and 18 years old at the time, had their own rooms, too. My mother always wanted me to be the last one to use the bathroom. I didn't like to be last so sometimes I would *catch* water in a bucket and take it to my room, where I washed myself. That bucket, which I had bought for that specific purpose, is still part of my possessions thirty years on. (They certainly don't make them like that anymore.) It has a new purpose though – it holds water to keep the air in my bedroom moist.

Within weeks of coming to England, I started to buy different household items, which I hid away in crevices and corners, under my mattress, just anywhere, where they would not be seen. As the weeks and months crept by, it became increasingly more difficult to hide things. I gave up and just put my new acquisitions wherever I could find a big enough space to squeeze them into. I had made up my mind during the journey from Heathrow on the day I arrived in England, that I wasn't going to live with my mother for very long.

I earned my own money from various sources whilst living at my mother's: I worked at the Albion Road Centre for handicapped people, at a factory packing boxes and the government gave me about £10 per week. I wasn't badly off financially and my mother knew it. She would sometimes ask me to pay towards the telephone bill, even though I didn't use it. But *for peace sake*, I occasionally gave a few pounds. I did pay rent and made a contribution towards the cost of food. I had no problems making these latter payments, so I handed over the money regularly without any ill feeling.

As I said before, I planned to leave my mother's place as soon as I could, but didn't know how to go about it. I didn't feel at home there and every day I became increasingly more uncomfortable. One day I overheard a telephone conversation my mother was having; she and the other person were discussing how financial assistance could be obtained to help care for a disabled child. I listened keenly with no guilty feelings because the conversation was about me, and after all, I had contributed to the telephone bill even though I never used the phone. I could not believe my luck – the route to freedom was being unveiled in my hearing. I decided to explore the channel my mother had identified in her telephone conversation in order to obtain the money I needed to help set up my own place. At that time my 18-year-old sister was applying for assistance to get her own place. If she was going to be successful, it would be easier for me, I reasoned. My disability was in my favour. I was quietly excited.

I asked my sister to get me one of the forms she had used to apply for her own place. "What do you want it for?" she snapped at me.

"The same damn thing you want it for," I snapped back angrily. My sister got me the form and one of the tenants in the house, whom I could trust to keep a secret, helped me fill it out. At first she was quite reluctant to assist me and said, "I don't think I can fill out the form."

"Yes you can." I reassured her.

My stepfather, somehow, overheard the exchange between the tenant and myself and told her to go ahead and help me. Later my mother found out and told the tenant not to have anything to do with me. But my stepfather was philosophical and wise. He said to my mum, "Let her go ahead. If she gets it, she gets it. And if she doesn't, she still has a roof over her head." It is because of situations like these that I have a soft spot for my stepfather. He has always looked out for me. I would not be surprised if he was the driving force behind my coming to England. But I guess I will never know.

***

That night, whilst lying in bed, my mind drifted into a deep dreamlike state. The thought of having my own place was uppermost in my mind. I began to appreciate more the importance of Harry's, my stepfather's, intervention in advancing the possibility of me achieving my dream. His words, "Let her go ahead. If she gets it, she gets it. And if she doesn't, she still has a roof over her head" were being repeated in my head like the words of an old Jim Reeves record I used to play again and again: "Thank you every morning for a new born day…" or something close to that. As I continued to reflect, my mental sat nav began bringing up pictures of Harry from long ago.

A grin pulled back the corners of my mouth as my mind started to play back the encounters I had had with my stepfather from those early days in Jamaica. The screen of my mind showed me standing in Charlotte's yard looking down on to the road. Depending on the time of day, there was a man walking on an east-west route, either going to his fields or returning to his home where he lived with his mother. Sometimes he would carry a bag with ground provisions, or a bunch of bananas or plantains, all destined for the cooking pot. Other times he held a fork with his left hand on his left shoulder and a machete in his right hand, swinging it rhythmically as he walked. Those early scenes depicted nothing spectacular about Mass Harry: he was just another subsistence farmer doing what most men did in the locality.

There was no reason to speak to him as my house was far enough away from the road to allow me just to observe the man's activities without requiring me to say 'hello.' As children, however, we would find our way to the homes in the neighbourhood as part of our leisure activities. Sometimes I would go to Mass Harry's home and if it so happened to be mealtime, his mother, Miss Mary, would always give me something to eat. I would not stay long after I had eaten, as there were no children of my age group there to play with. There were, however, two small children, babies really, but they were mostly in the house with their mother, Auntie Hecky. They did not relate much with me; neither did Mass Harry.

As it turned out, it was the same Auntie Hecky, Mass Harry and their two children who came to live with Charlotte and me in our house, before he left for England. Mass Harry did not treat me differently from his children. By then I knew he was my stepfather and (kind of) wished he was the father I did not have or know.

The term stepfather did not feature much in my mind then, until much later when he visited from England and decided that the condition I was living in was abysmal. To use his own words, "No, no you can't live like this" and right away he arranged for me to go and live with Aunt Ina.

Still in a dreamlike state, in the dark and lying on my back in my little room, the film had fast-forwarded from scenes in Jamaica to real time in London. Another set of my stepfather's quietly and deliberately spoken life changing words was on the screen: "Let her go ahead. If she gets it, she gets it. And if she doesn't, she still has a roof over her head." I felt my eyes well up with tears and the film was reset a little further back to the day I came to England.

My stepfather was not at home when we got in from Heathrow Airport. He came in after 6pm from work, hung his jacket on the back of the living room door, looked at me and uttered, "Welcome. Are you happy?" He then instinctively took a seat in front of the TV, not another word said, until Aunt Hecky called him for his dinner.

A week or so later I was in the safety of my room crying, when unexpectedly there was a knock on my door. "Come in," I said while trying to remove the evidence of tears from my face, but did not do a thorough job quickly enough to prevent my stepfather asking:

"What's wrong?" Before I could answer he said, "Are you happy?"

"No."

"Would you like to go back home?"

"No. I miss home and my son – David - but I don't want to go back now." I was surprised that I mentioned David's name. I'd tried to keep him in my mental pictures only, and would reluctantly speak about him if asked, and that was seldom. I was sure, though, that I did not want to go back now. Hard as it was, I had other plans, both for David and me.

"If you really want to go back let me know." That was the end of the visit. He just left the room without another word, pulling the door shut behind as if to say, 'Don't let anybody see you crying.'

I also recall reflecting on how well my stepfather and I got on:

He didn't single me out for any exceptional treatment but neither can I recall him being unkind to me. There were times when he would take me in his car to the shops or other places. When his friends asked him who I was he used to say, "This is my wife's daughter." After hearing him, the third time referring to me as his "wife's daughter," I decided to put an end to it. As we got into the car I said, "It would be better if you tell people that I'm your stepdaughter.' He simply said, "OK." And "my stepdaughter" is how he introduces me up to this day.

My stepfather was not into deep conversations. After work he would watch TV, mostly alone, before and after dinner, while my mother was always busy doing one thing or another. I would be in my room. He does not smoke, gamble or drink alcohol. He went to work religiously but did not discuss what he did in the factory. He goes to church every Saturday and although I didn't often see him, I knew he read the Bible in his bedroom every night. If there was an issue with my mother and me, he did not intervene.

I woke up the next morning a little tired from the late night at the 'movies'. I can't remember what was the last scene I saw, but I know it would not have been earth shaking or scary, because it was about my stepfather. Even now, years later, each time I speak with my mother, who is now living in Florida, my stepfather always has a word with me too. He always wants to know if I am happy.

***

Two years after submitting my application for independent accommodation, there was still no response from Hackney Council. I went to my GP and he wrote a letter to the council in support of my application. He advised me to get the help of my social worker to draw up a letter to send under my own name to the council. About six months later I got a response; someone from the Housing Department was going to visit me. I had not reckoned on a visit to my mother's house. And to make matters worse, I hadn't told her of any development since my stepfather effectively told her to let me be.

To help keep mum in the dark, I had worked out the time the postman would make his delivery and developed the practice of being the first person to pick up the post from the hallway. If for any reason the postman had to ring the bell, I was right there, ever present. Mum had never seen the letters from Hackney Council.

The housing representative came. I started on the way up to the third floor and made heavy work of the stairs, sitting down before the second floor to rest. Then between the second floor and the third, I went into the bathroom to get the key to my room. As we squeezed into my little room there on the third floor, the man stared as if he had seen a ghost. Every square inch of the room appeared to be occupied and boxes were stacked on top of each other. The little bed just fitted in the room, wall-to-wall, and there was just about enough floor space for both of us to stand without touching each other. He wrote a few things in his notebook and the only thing I remember him saying was, "No, you can't stay here." Those words were like music to my ears.

Within two weeks I got a letter from Hackney Housing Department offering me a one bedroom flat on Wrens Park Estate. My first thought wasn't jubilation at being able to leave my mother's house, but rather, how I was going to get my son David over from Jamaica, a secret ambition I had had all along.

I jerked out of my momentary daydream and started to plan my move in earnest. I already had most of what I needed for my new flat right there in my little room, so breaking the news to mum was going to be easy. She took it visibly well. No resistance at all. The few big items I needed were obtained quite quickly. My mum bought me one dining table chair, for which I was most grateful. Mr Yang, my boss at the Yang's health store, moved me to my new home. So three years after coming to England, having just turned 30, I was living under my own roof. The fact that it was rented wasn't a considered issue. The money I had paid towards telephone bills at my mother's had certainly brought multiple benefits, unintentionally.

When my mother came to my flat she remarked, "You are not going to be happy on your own."

"We'll see," I replied. She thought I would not manage. Even then she still didn't know me.

Over the years I tried to be a daughter to my mother. I visited her and she would visit me, particularly during the first three months of living on my own when I didn't have a telephone. She often asked me to come to her for dinner, but I seldom went.

After I felt I had established my independence, I did go for the occasional Sunday dinner. She tried to force me to take my clothes to wash in her washing machine. I never did. I washed everything by hand. For me that was no sacrifice. I had washed my clothes and those of others by hand for the better part of 26 years during my country-life existence in Jamaica. I bought my first washing machine in March 1983. To me that was sheer luxury.

In 1987, one year after my son David joined me in England, my mother moved for good to the sunshine state, Florida, in the United States of America. I visited her in 1998, 2000 and 2002. She now introduces me to her friends as "my daughter".

I am happy to be my real mother's daughter, particularly now that Charlotte has died. In a sense, I have had the best of both worlds: two mothers in the two countries I love, Jamaica and England. But in each home, in both countries, the centre of my earthly life has been my son, David.

Chapter FIVE

My Son, David

David has never discussed or even mentioned my disability to me and I have not raised it either. I suspect he has succumbed to society's interpretation of normality and consequently wore a mask of denial.

David was born on 31 March 1971 while I was living on my own in Kingston, Jamaica. I had moved to Kingston from Succeed, where I lived with my Aunt Ina, to facilitate easier access to the ante-natal clinic. It was Aunt Ina who made the arrangements for me, knowing I could not manage the journey from Manchester to Kingston on a regular basis with nowhere to stay after a long day at the clinic. A girl, Maggy, was sent to live with me, but she was neither company nor use to me. Most nights she left me on my own in pursuit of the bright city lights and would come back early in the morning. Within a few days she left but would occasionally return to sleep a night or two, apparently to see how I was doing.

I was very anxious not to have an April Fool's baby. With me being physically handicapped, to have an April Fool's baby in Jamaica would make his life doubly burdensome. People born in Jamaica on the 1st of April are often teased so badly that even the slightest human error on their part would be interpreted as normal for a Fool Day's child. But to be born of a physically handicapped mother, who is sometimes called 'fool-fool' herself, on Fool's Day would burden the child to such an extent that society would label him a psychological misfit – damaged. In an attempt to minimise the chance of giving birth to a fool's day child, I made sure I went to the hospital on Tuesday, 30ᵗʰ March. The nurse sent me home; she said I wasn't due to give birth yet.

Reluctantly I went home, but I made myself very active, physically, doing every and anything that remotely needed to be done. I danced and jumped around hoping that it would induce labour. I prayed, asking God not to let me have a Fool's day child. That night I stripped the bed of the sheets the landlady had provided and lined the mattress with all the newspaper I could find. Then I made my bed neatly with the sheets Aunt Ina had given me. I was getting ready to have my baby.

Wednesday morning, 31 March 1971: I was up early doing nothing in particular, and took a shower before breakfast. I sat on the bed-edge with a mug of 'cocoa tea', while Maggy sat on the chair having her breakfast. "Maggy," I said. She didn't stir or seem to notice that I had called her name. "Maggy," I repeated. This time she turned and looked in my direction. "Could you lend me some money?"

"What do you want it for?"

"Just in case I need to go to hospital and you aren't here." As the sentence leaves my lips I realise its implication and what Maggy's answer would be.

"No," she confirms with a stern voice. "The nurse said you are not ready to have the baby yet." I didn't comment further. I just sat there contemplating my next move.

It wasn't long after that that I got off the bed and put my empty mug in a green bowl on the table in a corner that had a few breakfast dishes waiting to be washed. I walked around the room making myself busy, rearranging anything that was slightly out of place or just paying close attention to some object in the room.

By 9.30am my waters had burst. I was in labour. I kept on walking around the room. Maggy noticed the trail of fluid and rushed outside returning with some newspaper to clean up the fluid from the floor. I kept on walking pounding my heels increasingly harder on the polished wooden floor. Maggy kept on cleaning up after me. Eventually she got quite angry, dropped what was in her hand on the floor and stormed out to the next room, to complain to Clarice about me. But I just kept on walking. I just about heard when Clarice said, "The baby is coming. Go and get the nurse!"

Maggy left at 1.30pm and returned after 6pm and shouted her message through a partly opened door: "The nurse says you must come in…" and she rushed off to the bathroom across the yard. When she returned the baby was crying and Clarice was beside me. Maggy just stood there in the doorway, staring at us, her eyes popping. Clarice said, "Don't just stand there. Go for the nurse!" Maggy turned and ran, returning in less than an hour, but this time with the nurse. Nurse Jones cut the umbilical cord and gave me an injection, before arranging for me to go to the maternity unit in the hospital van.

****

After Maggy had left me in the room the first time to fetch the nurse, the contractions became more frequent and intense. My bed was ready, so, alone, I took up the birthing position. I called on the experience I gained at the age of eight when I was in Kingston, living in hospital with other disabled children. Next door to the disabled children's day-school was a maternity unit, and, because there was shortage of staff, I was used as a 'go-fa' and allowed to talk with the mothers. The echo of "push!" during childbirth resonated in my ears. It was now my turn to push and I knew just what to expect – the expulsion of a baby. It did not bother me that I was alone giving birth. In this situation the phrase, 'Ignorance is bliss' is probably fitting.

The baby came out and I reached down and pulled him towards me. It was so good feeling the warmth of his body on my thigh. He gave out a shrill scream, and it wasn't long before Clarice came rushing in. "Pauline! Pauline! Oh my God! Are you alright!?" She rushed towards me and instinctively wrapped the baby in a sheet that I had placed on the bed for that purpose, then tended us both to the best of her ability. Clarice had just placed the baby beside me when Maggy came in and was immediately sent off the second time to get the nurse.

***

After two days, I left the hospital and went back to my room there in Kingston, where I stayed for another two days before Aunt Ina and her husband came for David and me. They took me in their car to live with them in their home in Succeed, Manchester, Jamaica. I was badly torn during the delivery, so I couldn't do much physical work during the first few weeks, but Aunt Ina looked after David and me as only a loving Jamaican aunt could.

I had my own big room and David slept in a cot in one corner, but many nights I took him into my bed because I just wanted to be near to him. I breast-fed David for nine months. Aunt Ina provided me with adequate food, so there was a good supply of breast milk to keep David nourished during that time. Occasionally, and more so towards the end of the nine-months of breast-feeding, I would supplement breast feed with the popular Cow & Gate formula and after eight months with cornmeal porridge and a pureed version of some of what I ate.

Before I got pregnant, I had looked after a number of babies in the village. Most of them started walking at about eleven months or older. David took his first steps at nine months. I didn't expect that. I just stood there and stared at him with a big grin and or open-mouthed expression. My automatic comment was, "Thank you Jesus. He hasn't got to go to hospital to learn to walk." (I had good reasons to be elated, as I'll explain later.) I ran outside where Aunt Ina was talking to someone and shouted, "Aunt Ina! Aunt Ina! David is normal - he's walking!" I could hardly believe what came out of my mouth. Up until then, no one knew of the agony I endured just worrying if my son would be normal. Aunt Ina just looked at me and smiled, knowingly and lovingly. What a relief!

I cared for David in the best way I could. He was a real lad – into everything. I had to wash him frequently because he seized every opportunity he could to play in the dirt outside. Sometimes I would spank him on his bottom or in the palm of his hand, but only after I told him three or four times not to touch dangerous objects. David would go with me to church on Sundays. I would carry him in my arms, which made me very tired. Sometimes my friend, Jane, would help me carry him to and from church. He would sit with me during the adult services, as I didn't want him to get pushed about by bigger children.

During the five and one half years I cared for my son in Jamaica, I was always 'Mummy' to him. There were no social barriers between mother and son. He didn't show any awareness of my disability. To his young mind, both of us were 'normal.' On one occasion, when he ran to greet me with a "mummy, mummy," excitement, an adult remarked, referring to me, "Look who wants the baby to call her mummy." I looked at the offender, society's *sample*, with what one might call 'an evil eye'. But I didn't care less what others thought! I was 'mum'! And a proud one too.

Leaving David in Jamaica before his sixth birthday was one of the most difficult things I had to do. It was more difficult than coping with society's taunts, abuse and ill-treatment. But leave him I had to. I didn't have a regular job, and money to look after my son properly was scarce. Aunt Ina did her best and she never once grumbled about providing for us.

When the invitation came for me to join my mother in England, I felt it was the best thing for both David and me. It was the opportunity I needed to establish myself, so that I could provide for him. I consoled myself, knowing that he was being left in good hands, and would be given the best that could be provided in the home of Aunt Ina. She had really cared for both of us. I didn't want to take David with me – not that there was an offer for him to accompany me to England. I wasn't sure what would happen in England. Going alone to explore possibilities was the only option.

Once in England, I further consoled and promised myself that I would write regularly and ask Aunt Ina to read my letters to David. I felt this was important to keep the bond between mother and son as strong as possible. I was determined that the miles apart would not dampen the relationship too much. But how was I to know? I was determined to send money as regularly as I could to assist with his care too, in the confidence that Aunt Ina would get whatever I sent.

When David was aged nine, I asked Aunt Ina to let him write to me. It was hard for him to write because he didn't have much to say. But every letter he built into a word meant much to me.

I took a keen interest in David's schooling. Aunt Ina kept me informed regularly and I got his school report every year. It was almost as if I was on spot. Each envelope that went with his school fees contained words of encouragement, urging him to work hard. I told him I was very proud of his achievements and that he should make the most of every opportunity, especially because I didn't have the chance to obtain a good education for myself.

In all my communication with my son, I said nothing about my disability. But Aunt Ina and other people had told him, so he was fully aware of my condition. David also knew his father, although there was no meaningful relationship between them.

Seven years after I came to England, I was back at the Norman Washington Manley International Airport in Kingston; this time with the sole purpose of seeing my eleven-year-old son. As I cleared customs and approached the meeting barrier, the first recognisable face I saw was David's. He was with Aunt Ina's husband. I heard David say, "There she is!" I rushed over and hugged him, leaving my luggage to look after itself. I eased David away from me, held him at arms' length; then we hugged again. We went to the car where David and I sat in the back.

The car had just about moved when the words, "I'm so glad to see …I missed you," came out of my mouth. I was excited but he didn't say much and we couldn't see any expressions on each other's faces in the darkness. We drove in the dark to Succeed. I was tired, but elated.

I stayed in Jamaica for three months. During this time I watched David's activities keenly. He had just won a scholarship (Eleven Plus) and was attending Knox College, where he was quite happy. I didn't visit his school, even though I wanted to, because I had his interests at heart and didn't want other children to tease him because of my disability.

The journey to school each morning was very hard. He would take the bus, when it ran, or any other transport that was going that way. There was no average time that he would arrive home. I was concerned about the lack of regularity in getting to and from school, but there was nothing I could do, at least not immediately.

David and I would have *hard* talks together, largely because I wasn't happy with his attitude towards Aunt Ina. He would ignore her when she called and seldom did what she asked. One day after such an incident, I said, "David, come here to me now." He came. "When Aunt Ina calls you, you must not ignore her. Go to her right now." He went. He soon realised that he could not play the fool with me.

The time came for me to return to England. We were both sad. In a way, it pleased me to see that the years and the chasm had not totally destroyed my influence on my son. But I was now, more than ever, determined to get David to England where I could be more influential in his life and give Aunt Ina a break.

Back in England I applied to the authorities for David to join me. The Home Office didn't want to hear. They thought I was living off the state and could not provide the financial support my son would need. I found out that the Home Office had written to my mum, who was still in England, to ascertain if she would guarantee financial support for David. It wasn't until I insisted on getting a reason for not giving me permission to have my son join me, that the Home Office relented and told me that my mother had refused to offer support for David to come to England.

I was livid. Vexed, I went to the Home Office. I engaged in conversation as soon as I sat down. "There is one question you have not asked me. You haven't asked me if I am working." They had assumed that because I am disabled, I wasn't working and was a burden on the

State. They asked me to provide proof of earnings. I there and then contacted my boss, Mr Yang, who spoke to the man at the Home Office, and gave verbal confirmation of my employment status, but they demanded it in writing, which was quite reasonable. The letter from the senior partner of Yang's Health Store begins:

"Miss Pauline Wiltshire has worked for this company in a variety of different duties on a part time basis for over 7 years and has shown herself to be capable of many tasks, and has had a position of responsibility and trust which she fulfilled with ample confidence. She shows intelligence and initiative in her attitude towards work…."

It wasn't long after the visit to the Home Office that a social worker visited David at Aunt Ina's home in Jamaica. Within two weeks of that visit, I got a telephone call from the Home Office advising me to start processing David's papers to join me. I smiled, realising that another hurdle had been cleared through the determination of this disabled frame. Another victory, but how many more were ahead was anybody's guess. Was anybody taking note that it might be a good idea to stop focusing on the outward appearance of the disabled person and instead take a little time to look at their abilities and human values? Medical and paramedical personnel are trained to deal with disabilities. Joe Public has no such expertise. So why do they waste their time focusing on my physical being when they cannot change what they are staring at? Might it not be better to give a helping hand across the road or just a smile?

Six months after the Home Office gave me the green light to process David's papers, I booked his seat at a travel agent in London. I wasn't going to take the chance of sending that amount of money home to Jamaica, particularly when I knew that David didn't want to come to England. I felt that at least, if he *stuck* out and refused to join me, I had control of my money.

David wrote and emphatically stated, "I don't want to come to England." It was time for me to tackle one of the most important hurdles in my life – getting my son to live with me, so we could bond as a proper mother and son. But I could not tell him that; I didn't know what psychological barriers he had developed as a consequence of my disability. I knew society was cruel and would not help me with this one, so I approached the problem from a humanitarian perspective.

I explained to David that he was a big boy now with intelligence to make the right decision for himself. I assured him that I would not force him to come to England, but that he should consider my reasons for wanting him to come. Once I got him to believe that he was in charge of the decision to come to England, I made my move. I reminded him that Aunt Ina's blood pressure was high, which made her quite ill. Also, because he was an active and strong young man, Aunt Ina could not manage him anymore and that it was only fair to give her a rest.

David was fully aware that I knew that Aunt Ina wasn't happy with some of his youthful antics. I assured him that it would take no time at all for him to make friends in England and that he would go to a good school every day on a regular school bus. I made the case for him to come to England, and it wasn't long after that he reluctantly accepted. I thanked God for the good news and eagerly ticked off another hurdle that was almost cleared. David joined me in my one-bedroom flat on 19

July 1985 and in less than a year after that, we were moved to the two bedroom flat were I still live, and with no plans to go anywhere else.

Within days of David coming to England, my aunt-in-law, Paula, and I went to a local boys' secondary school in Clapton, London and negotiated a place for him. He was accepted. I went to only one parents evening. David didn't want me there. (I somehow expected the children in England would be more tolerant. But no, children are children wherever they are – they can be very mean!) At the parents' evening the teacher told me that David was very bright. I just listened. There were many questions bursting to come out but I didn't want to embarrass David or give the teacher a reason to treat him differently during school hours.

I understood David's apprehension at having me involved in his school life. I stayed away from further parents' evenings, sports' days or any school functions which parents were expected to attend. I knew society's young ones would be unkind to me – children are instinctively cruel and it was David who I wanted to benefit from a balanced psychological development and a good education. He was already my son. No one could take that away from me. Painful as it was, I let him get on with his school life, whilst I observed, as through a telescope.

David didn't discuss his school life with me. Neither did he consult me about his options or further studies. But I secretly monitored his work with a periodic peek into his books. I was assured that he was making good progress. I was satisfied. After secondary school, David went to what is now Middlesex University and graduated with a degree in Computer Engineering. He left home at the age of 24.

David has never discussed or even mentioned my disability to me and I have not raised it either. I suspect he has succumbed to society's interpretation of normality and consequently wore a mask of denial. I often wondered how he felt. When Aunt Ina died he said, "My mum died." I wasn't hurt. Neither did I wish to deny him any meaningful grieving. In a way, he was right. Aunt Ina had cared for both of us. And David knew no other home from birth but hers, until he joined me in England, aged 14 years.

My experience with David has equipped me with skills to help other disabled mothers to cope. I used to go to the 'Centre' and advise them how to show their own mothers that they can manage. I advised them how to fend off their grandmothers who tried to run their lives for them, and encouraged them to be as independent as they could in caring for and showing love for their children. I reminded them that others would see their disability but seldom the need for a mother and child to bond. I emphasized that being independent does not mean doing everything by yourself, but rather it is doing what you can do for your child, and knowing when and where to seek assistance with those things that you cannot manage.

In my opinion, the disabled mother should ensure that they get home schooling for their children before they start nursery. This way the child's intelligence will surprise society and give the child a better start in life, thus limiting the baggage of society's handicapped view of disability.

David's friends, even now, relate to me well and often better than he does. He and I speak on the telephone about once each month and he visits me twice each year. When I miss David, I phone him and ask, "How is my son doing?"

"I'm fine," he answers. "I'm fine."

The love I give David, I never had. He knows his dad. I still don't know mine.

I really am proud of my son David.

Chapter SIX

Bringing Up Children

David's problems were compounded by the fact he had to get to know me, his mother, again. I was a stranger to him. What is more, his new home was in a foreign country with a different climate and very different customs.

Bringing up children in any era has never been the easiest of vocations. But being a disabled parent would compound the difficulties *many-fold*. Being born disabled and having had a normal child of my own have placed me on both sides of the counter. This has enabled me to take a balanced and practical look at what people, who find themselves in situations like I have, do face.

Leaving my son in Jamaica at age five and a half, when the relationship between us was healthy, and the attempts to re-establish that relationship years later, presented mega difficulties. David joined me in his early teens. This is not an easy age even for someone who has lived with his parents in one cultural setting all his life. David's problems were compounded by the fact he had to get to know me, his mother, again. I was a stranger to him. What is more, his new home was in a foreign country with a different climate and very different customs.

I was able to utilise the practical experience I gained through the varied situations my son and I lived through, to help other mothers in bringing up their children. No, I have not studied child psychology or read any books on child rearing, but my situation forced me to think through problems and come up with my own solutions, which may or may not agree with those psychologists use.

Below, I have strung together some unconnected *bits* that partially reflect my situation, thought processes and solutions to bringing up children. I have shared some of these ideas with disabled mothers when I worked with them, encouraging them to be sensibly independent for the betterment of theirs and their child's well being. The reader is free to eliminate any idea s/he does not agree with, or fill in any perceived gaps:

'When a parent leaves his or her child in the care of others and years later seeks to establish meaningful relationship with that child, it will not be the same as when parent and child live together from babyhood to late teens.'

'My son and I are complete strangers. Sometimes I try to speak with him but he doesn't answer. 'Other times, once in a blue moon, he'll come and speak with me.

'He behaves badly to me while with strangers he's very polite. I guess in his mind he's saying "I don't know her as a mother". So he takes out his frustration on me. I just take

it as it comes, reasoning, he's young and doesn't understand what life is about yet.'

'When bringing up children some of the things that will cause a disaster are:

'Not having adequate and sufficient food, clothing and warmth, which could all lead to poor health: We must have some money to buy things for the children because this gives them pleasure.

'It is sad when a family suffers for lack of the basics.

'Poor people do not get poorer by having children. They get poorer by not having enough support. It is no fun to have children when you are poor. And it is much harder if you are on your own.

'There is an extra worry if you can't control the child.

Bringing up children is too much for one person. The fun and joy of the child is lost.

'Some people have children and do not care for them.

'When the child is young you need to look after him/her properly and give him/her lots of support.'

'Some children grow up to hate their parents because they were provoked too much by them. It is bad enough when strangers provoke you, but it is worse when your family do it.'

'Some parents interfere too much in their adult children's lives.'

'The majority of parents who have disabled children find it hard to cope with them.'

'I would advise disabled parents not to leave their child in another country. Not even with their own family.'

Because of the way things have turned out between David and me, I have warned other disabled parents not to do what I did – leaving their child with someone else for years. It's not worth the long term pain and problems.

'It is better for disabled parents to live independently of their own family, particularly when they have children of their own. I was able to run my home and look after my child the way I wanted to. If I were living with my mother she would take over my life, including how my son should be brought up.'

'My mother never knew me or tried to understand me. She never knew who I was or what I'm capable of doing.

'Over the years my family have gradually come to understand what I can and can't do. By then my son had grown up, flown the nest and got his degree.'

David might not attribute much of his success to me but he came from a caring, supportive and loving home. That is a good start for bringing up children.

Chapter SEVEN

Falling In and Out of Love

That evening, Edward made his feelings for me known. I didn't resent it. After all, Caleb was off the scene and my love life had a vacant compartment. From then on, Edward looked after me royally.

It is generally perceived that a disabled person hasn't got a love life or hasn't got the capacity to love. Love is a feeling which is controlled by the brain and the heart and can envelop the whole body by way of the nervous system. Love ultimately manifests itself through the expression of touch and the sex organs. Since I have a brain, a heart, a sex organ, breasts and the sense of touch, I have the capacity to love. The shape of my body should not be seen as a determinant of my ability to love. The nerves are in tact, even though they may take abnormal routes, but they are in tact, so I can love.

I was about nine years old when I had what I thought was my first sexual urge. It was not connected to or directed at anyone in particular. It was just a warm glowing feeling in my chest, which I interpreted as being sexual. Maybe I was confused. It was not until after my first period at 13 that I felt unmistakably strong sexual urges.

Talking of my period, no one had told me what to expect. I didn't know such things happened to people. I was at school, sitting down in class, when I felt wet. I continued to sit there and would not move. During the morning recess, my male teacher saw me sitting alone in the classroom and asked, "How come you are not out playing?" I didn't answer him. He went and fetched his wife, also a teacher, and she sat beside me and enquired, "What's wrong Pauline?" I just pointed to my tummy.

Within seconds the rest of the class was in. The teacher, recognising what the matter was, sent the class outside to read under the broadleaf tree. Once the children were out, she took a safety pin from her dress and pinned up mine to hide the red stained spot. She cleaned the bench and took me to her home, which were only a few hundreds yards away. I was given a change of clothes, a sanitary towel and a few extra. Miss then sat me down and explained why I was bleeding and said that it would come every month. I gasped. She went on to say that when that happens, "Boys will want to go with you." She made it clear that I was turning into a lady, and *all* ladies bleed every month. (I do not recall if there was any connection between knowing that "boys will want to go with me" and my first unmistakable sexual urge, but the two were sequential.)

I felt special just to know that I was numbered among the ladies – all my female teachers were certainly ladies. But the thought of that experience, or a variation of it, happening every month filled me with horror! One thing for sure, the thoughtfulness with which one lady female teacher explained my monthly cycle to me, made me realise with a little less trepidation, that I had to live with it.

At the age of 10 or 11, a grown man made advances at me. He exposed his genitals and asked me to follow him to the outside toilet. I gave him a firm, "No." I was a bit angry - I wasn't ready for sex. He was a frequent visitor to Charlotte's house and whenever he got the chance he would bother me. One day he and I were in the outside kitchen, alone by the open fire where we cooked our meals. He held on to me and was pulling me towards him. I grabbed a live fire stick from under the pot and hit him in his crutch with it. He screamed when the fire burned him, but no one heard because Charlotte was sick in bed and out of reach. I told the man's elderly mother what he had done, but she just said, "You are a child and my son is a big man; he is a friend of the family, so he wouldn't ever do that to you." I was disappointed and silently resolved to look after myself and if necessary, use the fire-stick again. He didn't bother me after that.

The first time a boy took a real interest in me happened when I was 14. Tim was sitting on a pile of lumber in the yard when he said, "Just because you are handicapped doesn't mean that people don't have feelings for you. I do. And I love you." He was 20 years old, and it took about twelve months after that first encounter for the relationship to flourish. I was 15 and he 21 when Tim took my virginity. I had a steady relationship with Tim for about five years. We loved each other very much. I used to visit his parents who were very kind to me.

One Sunday, Tim was riding his bicycle on his way to see me, when a car knocked him down and killed him on the spot. He was 25 and I was 19. I was absolutely devastated. My first love had died coming to see me. I attended the funeral but could not stay. It was too much to bear; too hard to control my tears and I didn't want everyone to know that we were lovers. (Even now I still think of Tim with warm feelings.)

After Tim's death, other men tried to get my interest but I took no notice of them. I used to be the 'watchman' for my uncle's (Aunt Ina's husband) lumber which was piled up in the front yard. I would sit in the yard just to be visible to prevent the lumber being stolen. There was this man who was at least 55 years old, who came to talk to me on a regular basis. In a sense, we became two-watchmen, but he was not official. He would often steer the conversation to sexual matters, but I simply wasn't interested.

One day I was in the house alone, on my knees cleaning the front room floor. I didn't hear him enter the house. Certainly no one came through the front door. But all of a sudden I was grabbed from behind. There was a struggle, but I was no match for this man. He raped me.

After he did it, he said, just as if he had just conquered Mount Everest, "I got you now."

"You should not have done that," I said quietly but deliberate. I was trembling.

"Well, I don't see anybody trying to go with you, so I take it" - Yet more revelation that for him Mount Everest was conquered. He left the room by the front door while I sat there on the floor where he left me, feeling ashamed and dirty, wondering what to do next.

I told Aunt Ina, but because the man was always in the yard talking to me while I watched the lumber, she didn't believe my story. I told my friend Jane.

"That Dick is such a dirty old man," she said visibly upset.

It wasn't long after the rape that I realised that I was pregnant. I was worried about what people would say. I didn't have a job, no money, and Dick could not even help himself. The most difficult thing I knew I would have to cope with was the fact that people would say, 'She's handicapped and the baby will come out handicapped too'. I considered abortion but that seemed an unforgivable evil back then. Eventually, I decided to just accept my situation. I would have the baby.

Jane was the first person I told I was pregnant. She advised me to tell Aunt Ina. I did, but she still didn't believe me. Aunt Ina repeated her line, "He would not do that. He's a family friend." I went to the doctor and he sent for Aunt Ina and told her that I was pregnant. It was then that she started to show some concern.

In front of the doctor she asked, "What are you going to do now?" I guess she realised there would be an extra mouth to feed.

"I've been telling you for a long time now that this man was bothering me, but you took no notice. I am going to have this child." I said defiantly.

People started to talk. They said some hurtful things.

"The baby will come out fool-fool like her."

"She might die in childbirth."

"I wonder which man give her that baby?"

There were speculation and name-calling, but only Jane and Aunt Ina knew my true situation, at least as to who the rapist was and I wasn't going to tell anyone else. For me, this wasn't a hard secret to keep.

It became fixed in my mind, from overhearing some women talking about me in my apparent absence, that if a woman didn't have sexual intercourse during pregnancy, she would have a difficult birth. I didn't want any unnecessary difficulties during childbirth, so I called Dick, the man who had raped me, and made sure he became my sexual partner. As far as my pregnancy was concerned, this was by far the easiest task I had to do – there was no resistance from Dick. This arrangement between Dick and me continued up to two weeks before giving birth. Dick had brought my bed to Kingston and while I was waiting for labour to set in, we had sex.

Apart from the inevitable morning sickness, I had a trouble free pregnancy. My diet didn't vary, except that my appetite was very healthy. There was no need for me to take any unusual precautions to limit my normal activities.

After David was born, Dick tried to rekindle the relationship. I refused him. His duty was finished. This decision was easy for me to take, as Dick was going with too many women and I was even forced to have an argument with him each time I wanted a pint of milk from his own milking cows for the child.

One day I approached Dick, "Now you have a child, what are you going to do for him?"

"It isn't my child. It's the minister's. Let the church mind him." I was angry and determined that he would give me a pint of milk for the baby. I nagged him so much that he finally gave in.

Another day Aunt Ina sent for Dick and asked him to provide for the baby. Dick looked stunned. Aunt Ina asked him, "Dick, who does the baby look like?"

Dick uttered not a word. For David is a picture image of his father.

After Dick, I didn't have another sexual relationship in Jamaica. I left for England when David was five and a half years old. England was to turn up some unexpected surprises.

I wasn't looking for love in London. That was farthest from my mind. I was too busy trying to get my own flat and devising ways to get David to join me. But while I was with my mother, having a hard time, I often thought it would be nice if someone would come and take me out of the mess.

"Miss! Miss!" I had just got off the bus coming from the Albion Centre and had walked only a few hundred yards when I heard the voice calling. I looked and saw a man spraying cars on the forecourt of a house. I walked on without acknowledging the source of the sound. For about three months the man tried to engage me in conversation with his introductory, "Miss! Miss!" Often he would down his tools when he was rubbing down the cars and come closer to the pavement. He would make various comments as he stood and watched me pass by. The unrelenting "Miss! Miss!" and other comments from this man started to annoy me. I decided to take another route home from the Centre. It meant I had to walk for longer to get home when I got off the bus, but the uncomfortableness of the longer journey on foot was something my legs could easily cope with, rather than my ears and mind trying to adjust to the annoying "Miss! Miss!" from that man's mouth.

One afternoon I missed the bus on the longer route and had to take one that required me to walk past the "Miss! Miss!" man. As I got off the bus and walked the few hundred yards, to my surprise the man was there waiting. I pretended I didn't see him but couldn't ignore that irksome "Miss! Miss!" 'bird-call'. I took a slight glance in the direction, only to find the man walking right beside me. I walked on.

"You no hear me calling you?"

"No," came my deliberate response.

"Where have you been? I haven't seen you for a looong time." The tone of his voice told me that he was in search of something and that he wanted a response.

"I was somewhere else." I kept my head straight, not wanting to encourage too much dialogue.

"Well this time I find you and am not going to lose you. Where do you work?" He was insistent.

"I go to the day centre." I felt I had to at least be civil.

"Okay." And he turned back without saying another word. For about a month I made sure I was on time for the bus that took me the long route home. I just didn't want to hear that irritating "Miss, Miss."

It was a Tuesday afternoon and I had just emerged from the Albion Road Centre. He approached me as if he had triumphantly spotted his treasure-hunt prize. "Oh! So this is where you're hiding." By now he was standing right in front of me. I couldn't walk past this time and pretend I didn't see or hear him.

"I'm not hiding! How did you find me?" I retorted, contradicting myself in the same breath.

"I asked around for the Day Centre. Now that I know where it is, I'm not going to lose you," he said as we walked to the bus stop.

It wasn't long before the bus came. We got on the bus that took me the more direct route to my mother's house, which passed the man's workplace. I was hoping not to reveal the avoidance route I had taken over the past month. My pursuer was ready to pay my fare. I let him. As I got off at the other end and walked past the house where the "Miss! Miss!" call had come from, I found myself instinctively looking into the yard, but the sound-maker was right beside me. I looked up at him to find a wide grin on his face.

I made my way to the post office while he waited outside until I finished what I was doing. I then decided to do some window-shopping for a pair of shoes. He was behind or at my side all the way. He said very little, but scrutinised the shoes through the window with a more fixed gaze than a cat getting ready to pounce on a baby rabbit in a field. He interrupted the silence with, "Stop looking and go inside."

"I can't. I don't have enough money."

"Just go in and pick what you want." His voice was calmly reassuring. I thought about it. The shoes I had on were in a sorry state; the heels were lopsided and holes were in the soles. I went in and chose a pair of black lace-up shoes. He paid for them and followed me home.

On the way to my mother's house, the man surprised me by revealing at least one reason why he had been searching for me. In a slightly subdued tone he said, "I tried to find you because I didn't like what you had on. Your clothes and shoes didn't look good." He was right. My clothes didn't fit well and the hand-me-down coat was huge on me. As we got closer to the front steps of my mother's house, he said, "I want to help you." And without saying much else, he turned and left.

I knew my stepfather had seen us through the front window. He didn't say anything to me about my companion when I got into the house. But when my mother came home, I overheard him telling her, "I saw this dirty old man talking to Pauline outside the house." Later my mother came into the sitting room where I was watching TV.

"Pauline, Daddy said he saw you talking to a man outside."

"Yes, Mama. So what?" I was 27 years old and in a defensive mood.

"I would like to meet him."

"One day you will, but not right now."

The exchange with my mother caused me to think more about my newfound friend. He was tall and quite thin, and his appearance gave the impression that he wasn't taking good care of himself. My mother obviously thought he wasn't right for me. I later discovered that Caleb was living by himself in a rented room with the usual shared kitchen and bathroom facilities. Most days Caleb would meet me at Albion Road or somewhere else we had pre-arranged. It took a year before I visited Caleb's room and another six months before we made love. The relationship lasted from 1977 to 1982, by which time I was living in my own flat.

My sister was with me as I walked home, on a Tuesday afternoon, from the factory where I was then working. It was dark and we walked holding hands. We had just passed the bus stop when I heard Caleb's voice calling from behind. It wasn't "Miss! Miss!" anymore, but "Pauline! Pauline!" By then the relationship between Caleb and myself was a little strained. I said to my sister, "Keep on walking."

"Who is that?" Caleb enquired with a firm voice.

"This is my sister." I answered and kept on walking.

From then on Caleb became very jealous, but I wasn't sure about what. He didn't hide his feelings.

A week or so before I went to Jamaica in 1982, Caleb telephoned me. "I have some money for you." I didn't show any interest in his money but asked, "Can you look after my flat when I am away?" He agreed. When it was time to go, I called Caleb to come and collect the key to my flat. But to my surprise he queried,

"Why should I leave my place to look after yours?"

"That's okay, I'll get somebody else." And I put the receiver down.

The day after I returned from Jamaica, the telephone rang. "Where's my rum?" It was Caleb.

"Did you give me any money to buy rum? Furthermore, you didn't look after my place when I was away." I wasn't going to let him forget it. Our relationship slid further downhill after that.

From the time I lived at my mum's, Edward would drop me home from various functions. There were no mutual feelings between us, but I knew he fancied me even though he'd never said so. A woman, even a disabled one, knows. At times when Edward visited me, we would talk about Caleb. Edward always listened sympathetically and never said an unkind word about him.

When I told Edward that Caleb and I had broken up, he spontaneously replied, "Good." That was so uncharacteristic of Edward that I was a little stunned. After that Edward's visits became more frequent and he stayed longer. I wanted to know what he was thinking, so one evening, while we were having a cup of tea together, I asked, "Edward, why do you come here so often?"

Before he could answer I slipped in another question. "What about your wife?"

"Oh, don't talk about her." He became very uncomfortable. Restless even. My questions to Edward were not just to find out what he was thinking or to confirm any interest I may have assumed he had in me. There were a number of rumours that he was having difficulty with his marriage. His frequent and prolonged visits to my place told me that he was certainly not happy at home. No man with a healthy relationship would visit another person so frequently and start to assume a 'man-a-yard' posture. Also, added to my reasons for quizzing Edward was the knowledge that it was his wife who often told him to give me a lift home from the various functions that we attended together. Was she being a 'good Samaritan' or was she subtly creating a distraction from her marriage woes?

On one of Edward's visits, as he sat relaxingly and deep in thought in my easy chair, he said, "I'm not very happy at home…."

I listened as he disclosed some petty reasons for his declared unhappiness. He sounded almost childish, but I knew there were deeper issues, and what he had said was just a smoke screen, perhaps partly to test my reaction.

"Try and make up with her." I encouraged him.

"No. I've been trying for fourteen years."

That evening, Edward made his feelings for me known. I didn't resent it. After all, Caleb was off the scene and my love life had a vacant compartment. From then on, Edward looked after me royally. He bought me anything I wanted. We would go out in a limited way because we didn't want to draw attention to the new status of our relationship. My home was the nest for our romance. It provided almost legitimised closed doors for our romance to mushroom. He would always say a double love line to me: "I love you darling. I love you." I returned his love and deep affection. We were blissfully happy together. I had no guilty feelings. By his own confession, I wasn't depriving Edward's wife of anything. Things went on at his marital home much as they had done for the previous fourteen years.

There was, however, a change in my home. Edward had come out of himself and was a new man. He helped me to wash my hair, mend my clothes; he fixed my door and anything else that needed fixing. He would often join me in the kitchen and we would cook together. Edward wanted to share every part of my life and we did so with ease.

Out of the blue, after one of his silent thoughtful periods, Edward got up out of the easy chair, entered the kitchen where I was making tea, hugged me from behind and whispered in my ear, "I wish your son was mine." A warm glow enveloped me. I held onto his arms as they crossed my chest. I knew then if I could have more children, we would have one together – a lovechild. Our silence spoke more than any words or music could reveal. Edward being twenty years my senior made no difference. We were in love. Real love.

We were restricted by how long we could stay together - at night or whenever Edward dropped me home. We lived for those days when Edward's wife was away at her many weekend conferences, or out of the country on holiday with her friends. At those times he was all mine. During one of those times alone, Edward told me that his wife had once said, "I don't care what kind of woman you go with, so long as she isn't a disabled one." She certainly conformed to society's norms. A disabled woman was a lesser woman. Yet there I was, physically disabled and giving this man the time of his life. Our sex life was incredible and satisfying. He told me he had never been so happy in the past fourteen years.

Our relationship reached its zenith fairly soon after it got serious, and it never waned. It was only when Edward took ill that we did not see each other on a weekly basis. Of course I couldn't visit him at his home. I wasn't that bold.

When Edward died, I felt a part of me began to ebb away. I was distressed for many weeks. I didn't go to the funeral. It was too hard to bear. But the worst thing was that I couldn't send a card or a bouquet of flowers to anyone. I couldn't share my grief with anyone who knew Edward. I felt lost, dejected and disorientated. I cried both day and night. It was only the walls of my flat and a close friend who knew how I felt. My flat shielded me from the public's watch. And the friend could only provide limited consolation.

I have not really recovered from those losses – the loss of my first young love, who died tragically in a car crash on his way to see me, and the loss of Edward, my mature, true love. I don't want anyone else in my life. No romantic human love. Not another chance to fall in and out of love. Or rather, to have love snatched from me by the grim reaper – death. I had a choice and I have taken it. I decided to immerse myself in my church. That is the best relationship for me now. '*On Christ the solid rock I stand. All other ground is sinking sand.*' That is my decision.

Chapter EIGHT

My Christian Experience –
An Uneven Road

I felt the same good feelings I experienced when I was baptised in Jamaica. To me, both experiences were 'real'. The second time, I was only growing in Christ, and making the choice the Anglican minister had given me those many years before.

My earliest recollection of the concept of God is when I was five. I grew up in a Christian home and Charlotte took me to the local Anglican Church from the time I was nine months old until I was twelve; with the exception of when I was away in Kingston. Charlotte carried me to church until I was five (during this time my *legs of iron* were developing, at least mentally) when I could walk, but before that she always encouraged me to help myself in all situations. She would often say, "The only way you are going to help yourself is by relying on

God. When you go to church you will learn a lot about God and how he can help you."

Charlotte's encouragement still occupies my mind. Her emphasis on self-help, through God, was a potent self-development medicine. "Not because you are a handicap that you are going to sit down and do nothing for yourself." She often said.

Her words meant much to me in my early years when every other child around me was walking and I could only shuffle on the ground, or pivot on my right big toe, which was very painful. Charlotte made sure that I realised the reality of my situation though, "Other people would lock you away in a cupboard, but I won't. I want you to learn to pray to God and to help yourself."

Looking back, those early inspirational talks from the person whom I thought was my mother, instilled in me a fighting-spirit, the determination to help myself in any situation. God had certainly arranged the right home for me in which to develop a positive self-image, self-esteem and the desire to live.

Each Sunday, Charlotte would carry me the one and a half miles to church. When she got tired, she would transfer me from one side to the other. Occasionally we would get a lift in a church member's car. Even when I could walk by myself, after corrective operations in Kingston, it was still a difficult journey. I got very tired and frustrated, walking with tremendous difficulty in a rise and fall manner, the whole distance from home to church and back, but I kept going because I believed God was going to do something for me. To be honest, I mostly kept going to church because Charlotte encouraged me.

At Sunday school, they would read stories from the Bible and ask questions. The Sunday school teacher would allow me to answer some of the questions, even though it was difficult for them to understand what I was saying. I was very happy in the class and each time I was allowed to answer a question it gave me great joy. I would listen quietly to the preacher during the adult's service, but I got very expressive during the singing, clapping my hands and moving my body a bit, even though that wasn't the norm in the Anglican Church. I made a 'joyful noise' anyhow, as they say; well, some would say.

The adults would always recite the Lord's Prayer, but the first prayer I learnt started 'Gentle Jesus meek and mild, look upon this little child…." And that's all I could ever remember. But every night before going to sleep I'd pray, "In my little bed I lie, heavenly father hear my cry, Lord protect me through the night, keep me safe 'til morning light."

When it dawned on me that God was watching over me, and that he cared for little children, it really made me very happy. As I grew older and learnt to repeat the Lord's Prayer, it took on major significance in my life. It was comforting to know that I had a father, somewhere, who cared for me. I was thankful that He provided Charlotte with some food and gave her strength to look after me.

Taking part in church was very important to me. Even though walking was very painful, I wouldn't think of missing a single Sunday in church. As I got older I would listen keenly to the sermons, which triggered many questions in my mind. I would sometimes ask the minister or a deacon after the service to explain things I didn't understand.

"You said Jesus is coming soon. *When* is he coming?"

My life wasn't exactly pretty and people were making fun of me; so if Jesus came, I reasoned, I would have a better life.

One Sunday after church, I asked the minister, "The Bible says Saturday is the Sabbath. How comes you are preaching on Sunday?" He was taken aback by my question.

"There are many religions and it's up to you to choose which one you like," he responded uncomfortably.

I kept going to the Anglican church until I was almost thirteen when I had to move from the area to live with my aunt.

When I was nine I had a long spell away from that church. It had nothing to do with any doctrinal disagreement; Charlotte was in her 70's and was very ill so I had to stay home to look after her. I didn't even go to school. The other two girls (mother and daughter) whom Charlotte raised weren't very helpful. The mother was always fussing with anybody who entered her space. At that time most of the household chores fell on me.

My stepfather's brother was living only a sort distance from me, in the same place as my real mother used to live, before I knew she was my mother. After two years of staying at home looking after Charlotte, I became desperate. There was very little food, my clothes were not of the best and household chores seemed to increase on a daily basis. Water had to be carried from the river, the yard swept, the house cleaned, fire wood collected to cook the little food we could find, and Charlotte's other 'adopted' daughter and granddaughter were no *earthly good*. By this time I was eleven and mature above my years. Still unable to go to church or school, I mustered up the courage to go and see Uncle Willie, my stepfather's brother.

Uncle Willie was a truck driver and he liked his drink. As I approached his house I called, "Hold dog," as was the custom to say when going into anyone's yard.

He shouted back, "Who is that?" Unbelievable! My voice was unmistakable. How could he not know who it was? Had he merely raised his head from off his chest, he would have seen the unmistakable me, with my rising and falling gait coming up his drive. I walked onto his veranda.

"Good day Uncle Willie."

"What you want gal?"

I paused and decided to get straight to the point.

"Uncle Willie, if you weren't drinking so much you would see what is happening to me and you would take notice of things in my life. Can you write to your brother in England and tell him about my condition? Tell him that I have no money, no clothes, nothing!"

I couldn't write to my mother myself, as I didn't have her address. But I felt that if God was going to look after me, as Charlotte had always told me he would, then that help would most likely come from England, and it was time I did my part – giving God something to bless.

A year after I went to see Uncle Willie, my stepfather visited Jamaica and stayed at his brother's at Mason Run. Within a day he came over to Charlotte's house. I was bathing her in a bath pan at the time. I didn't know how long he stood there watching me, without my knowledge. But when I saw him he began walking slowly towards us. We chatted, mostly he and Charlotte. His stay wasn't long. But before he went he spoke directly to me, "I can't let you stay here like this. I'll see what your Aunt Ina can do."

The next day Aunt Ina came for me to live with her. It was hard leaving Mama, but I wasn't given a choice. The few things I had were packed into a little cardboard box and placed on the back seat of the car with me. I gazed through the window and watched the trees running by as if they were on legs.

Aunt Ina was a Moravian and went to church regularly on Sundays. She was very active in her church and as a primary school teacher she seemed to know every child's name there. Her church was just about half a mile from where she lived. I would attend when she took me, which wasn't very often, and at special functions such as harvest festivals and concerts. I didn't like going to that church. I missed the Anglican congregation – they had known me since I was a baby. But that church was too far away for me to walk, and transport wasn't available.

I prayed to God for help. Things at Aunt Ina's were much more comfortable than at Charlotte's, but I felt the need to pray more. I did what Charlotte had taught me – prayed that God would help me to improve myself.

* * * *

Four years on, I was fifteen. It was a calm day, but I had this overpowering feeling, compelling me to go and see Mama. That night I dreamt seeing her. She asked me to visit her. The next day I asked Aunt Ina to take me there but she wanted to know why I was so eager to go and see Charlotte. I couldn't give a good clear reason so Aunt

Ina said no. I told myself, 'This is one rule I am going to break. I am going to see Mama'.

I stood at the bus stop, hoping for a miracle transport that would come to take me to see Mama. Just then, coming from the opposite direction was Sissy, one of the girls who lived with Charlotte.

"Pauline, it's you I come to look for. Charlotte is dead. For the last three days, every step she heard, she just keep looking to see if it was you. When she didn't see you come she said, 'Lord, take care of Pauline' and closed her eyes."

Sissy and I got to the house as quickly as we could, thanks to a van driver that was going in that direction. In the bedroom, I saw mama lying on the bed, stretched out. I gently removed the cover from her face, placed my head on her chest and wept. My sobbing was the only sound that could be heard. Sissy just stood there in the doorway with her head leant against it, and with ceramic-like gaze onto the floor.

At the funeral service I cried and couldn't stop. It got worst at the graveside. I rolled in the mud. One or two people held me. I don't know who they were, but tears were my only consolation. Mama had died. But her words of inspiration were riveted in my mind: "God will help you to help yourself."

There were occasional open-air meetings that were conducted by the Church of God on a piece of land near the road, not too far from Aunt Ina's house in Christiana. My friends would go into the meetings, but not me. I would just stand in the road and enjoy the singing. It wasn't long before they started to put up a church building. I would help to carry stones, just to make myself useful and to allay boredom. When the church was completed, I started to attend the meetings on occasional Sunday afternoons. The singing was great. I enjoyed it. The clapping and bobbing and weaving – worshipful dancing - helped me to express myself and to reach out of myself in praise to God. It was therapy for me. But even then, I delayed in joining the happy band of singers inside on a regular basis.

Eventually I relented and I gradually slipped into regular attendance at the Church of God and took part in everything I could. Just about the time I started to settle down, Aunt Ina moved house to Succeed and instinctively I attended the nearest Church of God meetings in Colville. Both Church of God congregations in Christiana and Colville were about the same distance from my new home. Ideally I would have liked to continue attending the one in Christiana, since I knew the people and was by then very happy there; but the ease of transportation to and from Colville made it more convenient to make it the one I attended regularly. It didn't take me long to settle into the new congregation. The singing and style of service was the same as in Christiana and I loved it.

The preacher at the Colville Church of God would often speak about the Sabbath. I found this a little confusing because he said Sunday was the Sabbath, but my reading of the Bible told me that Saturday, the seventh day, was the Sabbath. It was about this time that I started to take my relationship with God more seriously. I wasn't sure what to do about the question of whether Saturday or Sunday is Sabbath, I didn't know much more than what I read in the Bible. There was no question, however, about my happiness in the Colville Church of God congregation. I remembered what the Anglican minister had told me about deciding on which church to worship at. I reflected on my feelings, my relationship with people and most importantly with God. At the time, I believed Jesus was urging me to 'go into the water' and be baptised. There was this strong inner voice that said, 'Don't be afraid'.

I took the plunge and was baptised right there at Colville. I continued in the Colville congregation and soon lost any slight doubts as to whether I was in the right church or not. I was happy there and enjoyed the fellowship until I left Jamaica at the age of 26.

In London I looked around for a Church of God meeting place. The one I found wasn't that interesting. I didn't continue going there for long. At that time my mother regularly attended an Adventist church on Holloway Road every Saturday. I decided to go with her to see what it was like. It was August 1976 and it was very hot. I walked into the church and found a seat without any assistance. No one introduced me, as I was accustomed to in Jamaica. I just sat there. After the service a few individuals came over to where I was sitting and asked who my mother was. I just pointed to her a few rows ahead. You should have seen the surprise on their faces. One woman who could not contain herself retorted, "I didn't know she had an older daughter? I've known her all these years and she never mentioned you to me." I felt that my mother was ashamed of me. But there wasn't anything she or I could do about it now. We were mother and daughter.

I attended the Holloway Adventist church for six months. It was during that time that I started going to the Day Centre on Albion Road, in Stoke Newington. One afternoon I was walking along Osbaldeston Road, when a lady, whom I later knew to be Sister Roosevelt, engaged me in conversation and invited me to the Stoke Newington Seventh-day Adventist Church, which was only a mile from where I lived and was on a direct bus route. The following Saturday I went to the church in Stoke Newington instead. The people there were very friendly to me and I felt at home there.

It wasn't long before I started attending Bible studies on Friday evenings at Sister Roosevelt's home. This took me deeper and deeper into the Bible, and at last, the Sabbath question of many years ago was answered. My attendance at the Stoke Newington Adventist church became regular from 1978. I went to every evangelistic series of meetings, was regular at mid-week prayer meetings and took part in the services in any way I could. I particularly loved Sabbath School on Saturday mornings, where I could ask and answer questions on the Bible. I was happy in church again.

It wasn't until 1993 that I decided to commit my life more firmly to Jesus and worship him more meaningfully and without reservations. My life was more in tune with what I *believed* was true. Later that year I was baptised for the second time. But this time, in the Adventist church. I felt the same good feelings I experienced when I was baptised in Jamaica. To me, both experiences were 'real'. The second time, I was only *growing* in Christ, and making the choice the Anglican minister had given me those many years before.

Subsequent to my last baptism, I opened my home as a place where Bible studies could be held. Sometimes there are up to seven people in attendance. This helps me particularly during the winter months when I find it difficult to travel in the cold.

God gives me the confidence to cope with life's trials. He has provided for me much more than anyone could expect. On reflection, I have had many jobs that people thought would never come my way. I have looked after children in their homes and in mine. God has certainly been good to me, in spite of myself.

I pray in the mornings and at nights when I am alone. I pray at church in small groups. It is a good feeling talking to God, knowing that he cares. I will never forget Charlotte encouraging me to pray and ask God to help me to help myself. God has kept his side of the bargain.

I know God accepts me for who I am. He has forgiven me for the wrongs I have done. I'm assured that I should not worry about what people may say about me. I have no preconditions in serving God. I intend to just go on believing in God, my heavenly father.

I'm happy being a Christian even though people drive me mad sometimes. But I believe that I am in the right group, at the right place. I know that not everyone is physically, mentally or socially perfect. This helps me to develop tolerance. And God has watched over me during my Christian journey. It has been an uneven road, but I have grown.

Chapter NINE

Provocation

*P*rovocation came in different forms. People in the community were no better than any other. They called me names and made references to my biological parenthood in a snide way.

Like the English, Jamaicans can be found everywhere in the world. Jamaicans can be notorious as in the case of Yardies, but are actually better known for their reggae music, track and field excellence, (It is commonly held by Jamaicans, and others who are in the know, that if all Jamaicans in an Olympics where to represent Jamaica, the medal table would read quite differently), political achievements (as exemplified by Portia Simpson-Miller, Marcus Garvey and Colin Powell), as well as academic and religious achievements around the world. But there is something else Jamaicans are well known for: as a consequence of our particular brand of sense of humour, we are merciless at teasing, name-calling and making fun of others at their expense. In brief, Jamaicans are masters of provocation.

If the West Indies Cricket team does badly, Jamaicans do not need foreign journalists to write the obituary. We do it best for ourselves and the knife is usually very long and sharp. If any of our public personalities trip up, we give it to them the hardest. But we also give praise exuberantly and protect our own like the Englishman does.

The art of provocation is received-education from the earliest years at school. Names like, *Brok-up-Johnny* (a boy walking with a limp), *Puff-Jaw* (a girl with rounded cheeks), *John-Crow Parson* (a man walking around with a safety helmet), *Miss Dan's Sugar* (a child who stole Miss Dan's sugar) are just a few examples of what one could hear among seven-year-olds going home after school. These names are usually directed at whoever the caps fit.

In my case, there were countless names I had to endure: 'Fool-fool', 'Idiot', 'Water-mouth' and many more. There was no consideration given to the fact that I was *born* disabled and there was nothing I or anyone else could do about my disability status.

I became conscious of my disability when I was about four years old. Luckily for me, I noticed it before the name calling started. It first dawned on me that something was wrong when I had difficulty putting on my clothes. I could not work out what was wrong and so dressing became a most frustrating task. Other children around me would jump in and out of their clothes with ease, but for me it was a struggle.

Another thing that brought home the awareness of my situation more starkly was the way children walked differently from me. I couldn't walk properly, I pivoted on my big-toe, which was very painful, but it was the only way I could manage. The freedom other children had in moving around made me think that something was wrong with me. Other children's speech was different to mine, too. Their clothes fitted differently. I knew something was wrong with me.

I asked my mama, Charlotte, to explain why the other children walked, dressed and talked differently from me. She told me, "That's the way you were born."

Mama told me that one day I approached her and demanded that she made me walk like the other children. Her response was, "I'll see what I can do."

Mama took me to Spaulding Hospital and eventually I was sent to the university hospital in Kingston, where I stayed for four and a half years. My friends were now other disabled children, some older than me, some younger; some with less disability, others with greater. I became more confident when I saw many cases much worse than my own. But what built my confidence most was the fact that I was treated as being *normal*. There was no provocation or name-calling.

After I had the operation on my leg, it was put in a splint, and once that splint was removed, I was able to walk just a little better than before – I didn't have to pivot on my big toe any more. I was able to help both myself and others. And because I was treated in a kind way, I was ever so eager to help those who were worse off than me. I enjoyed the years spent in the hospital.

Except for those times when I was actively under treatment or in a splint, I went regularly to the school for the disabled at the hospital. I felt that the teachers valued me and I learned as fast as my disability would allow.

Charlotte would visit me every two weeks and sometimes took me home for weekends. I was lucky because many children's parents never visited them and the hospital was their permanent home. Although I was there with them, I was different. They'd become institutionalised from birth. I had a home.

At the age of eight I left the hospital and went back home to live with Mama. She enrolled me into a normal all-age school in Pike. I started in A-Class even though I was a year older than the entry age for that class. From day one, both the children and adults teased me mercilessly. Some of the children called me "Big-mouth," a fair name for I did defend myself verbally and wouldn't take their teasing lying down. Others would call me "Run-mouth," because I dribbled a lot. The children scorned me and it hurt.

In an attempt to keep order in the classroom, the teacher would put me to sit by myself in a corner. When she wasn't looking, I would get up and sit beside any child where there was a vacant seat. Sometimes I would push myself against a child to make space. This resulted in either me being pushed away or the child running away leaving a space beside the next child in the row, which I readily claimed.

My persistence in being part of the class and not being isolated soon wore them down. But it was when Devon befriended me and allowed me to sit beside her all the time that calm came to the classroom. Devon is still my friend today and she visits me regularly.

Although there was a semblance of calm in the classroom, the situation was quite different after school. Some of my classmates, together with older children from other classes, would join forces to call me all sorts of names and even threw stones at me. The stoning session would take place at a point where those involved changed directions for their homes. Luckily for me, another friend, Paulette, was always there for me. She would help me throw stones back at them. It was very satisfying when two other girls joined my team. We had to be good at throwing stones because I couldn't run fast. I was hit two or three times. But when my side was strengthened, the other side ran away under the concerted attack, laughing as they disappeared out of reach. It wasn't long after that that the stone throwing stopped.

Provocation came in different forms. People in the community were no better. They called me names and made references to my biological parenthood in a snide way. In church, one lady in particular felt she knew where I should sit when Charlotte was in the choir. On one occasion, when she put me in a corner and went back to her place in the choir, I got angry and stormed out. The lady tried to get me to go back but I just would not listen. I screamed and sat down on the floor when she grabbed my hand to pull me back to 'my place.'

Even though the stones hurt, one of the most painful forms of provocation came at the hands of people in my own home. They caused me a lot of problems. When I was at Aunt Ina's, in Jamaica, they would take things and say it was me. I used to get beatings because of Dell, who Aunt Ina brought to live with us while we were living in Succeed to provide me with some company. When chores were not done, it was always my fault. If I did mine and Dell didn't do hers, she would mess mine up and get me in trouble. I used to hate her for doing those things to me. The maid at Aunt Ina's would get the men to provoke me. However, there was one satisfying time when Aunt Ina found out that one of the maids set up a man to seduce me. I was fifteen at the time. Aunt Ina sacked her instantly. I put my head through the front window as she left and said in a voice loud enough that only she could hear, "Serves you right."

As I said earlier, provocation comes in different forms. For instance, several earlier attempts have been made to write this book. But each time my co-writers, all of whom were white, wanted to write my story from within their British experience, so the story contained very little evidence of the first 26 years of my life living in Jamaica. I got the impression they thought that because I am a black, disabled woman I shouldn't have strong views of what should be in my book. But those people didn't really know me and tried hard to 'walk all over me', but they soon realised that I will not be 'walked-over'.

Some of my worst experiences of provocation took place in England. One would expect that in a situation where racism abounds, a black disabled person would get a double whammy of discrimination.

When I was at the Albion Road Day Centre, the way the white staff spoke to the black disabled clients made me very angry. But the way the white staff treated the one black person who was on staff at that time was most disgraceful. While black disabled clients were treated much worse than white ones, I often wondered why the black staff member took all their psychological and verbal abuse. She was treated like dirt. I would not have put up with such nonsense.

The meals that were provided for clients at that time were made for the English palate. To me the meals were tasteless mush, without any seasoning. I dreaded mealtimes. On one particular occasion, I couldn't take it anymore, so I decided to get an alternative lunch. I obtained permission from the black member of staff, Mary, to go to the shops offsite. Mary asked me to get her something too and gave me the money. I left just before everyone sat down to eat.

When I returned and just as I got through the front door, a male staff member, Danny, grabbed me by the neck and said, "How many time have I told you not to go out?" I beckoned to one of the white trainees, that is what the clients were called, to take the lunch (which was in my left hand) from me. I said to Danny, "Now is the time to let me go."

Instead of letting go of my neck, Danny just shouted,

'Didn't I tell you not to go out?" He was hurting me and would not listen to my plea to stop strangling me, so I formed my left hand into as firm a fist as possible and hit him as hard as I could in his private parts. The clasp on my neck was instantly loosened. I said to Danny, "I am not Mary. I am a 27-year-old trainee," and walked away, leaving Danny doubled up with both hands forming a guard around where my fist had landed. He never bothered me again.

The staff at the Albion Road Centre used to take us away on residential trips for a week. I enjoyed those times away because they helped me to get to know and see more of Britain. One trip was to Devon.

Each staff member was responsible for five trainees. I lived on the same road as one of the white staff members who was very kind to me. She recognised that I was the most able among the trainees at the Centre and often said there should be 'somewhere else' for trainees with my level of ability. Unfortunately, I wasn't in her group on the Devon trip.

In my group, there were three black and two white trainees. I shared a room with Sarah, a white trainee. We would take turns to go to the shops, but Sarah couldn't go on her own, even when it was her turn.

Trainees were expected to make the beds of staff and provide cups of tea as and when they were required. It was Sarah's turn to go to the shops, but it was raining. As she would have needed a lot of help in the rain, it was decided that I should go to the shops alone for her. When I returned, Sarah was crying. I asked her what the matter was: Sarah informed me that Peggy, our staff-carer, was shouting at the black trainees and didn't speak to them in the same way she spoke to the white trainees. Sarah, who was well known for being very sensitive, was *really* upset. I asked her to explain what happened. She offered her observations readily: Peggy would say to the white trainees,

"Could you make my bed, please? Could you make me a cup of tea, please?" But when it came to the black trainees, it was, "Make me a cup of tea…. Make the bed." It became clear that Sarah had been noticing the difference for some time.

"Don't worry." I consoled her. "I will deal with her. Tomorrow it is my turn to make the beds."

The next day Peggy gave me the command, "Pauline, make my bed."

"I am *not* here to make your bed. Mine is already made." Peggy glared at me, clearly surprised.

"You are rude."

"I don't care. I am not going to do it." I knew Peggy didn't like black people, so I seized the opportunity to make my feelings known to her. "I don't like the way you treat black people. Black people *is shit* to you."

Peggy left and went next door where she complained to the other staff about me. Later that day, I met the staff member who liked me. She looked at me, smiled and said, "Good for you, Pauline." On the following day, while we were out walking, I telephoned my mother from the public phone box. Peggy, without asking, took the phone from me and spoke.

"Mrs whatever-your-name-is, your daughter is rude," and shoved the receiver back into my hand. When I got home, I told my mother that if she wanted to see what was going on, she should come down to the centre and I would show her.

My mother took up my invitation without telling me she was coming. I took her to the manager's office and ask one of the trainees to call Peggy. I outlined to the manager how Peggy had treated us and got some of the trainees to be witnesses. After that meeting Peggy did not speak to me for two years. I didn't care. At least I did not have to put up with her nonsense.

I left Albion Road to work in a factory when I was approaching 29. The first week I travelled with the staff from Albion Road who showed me the way. We would meet at Clapton Station at 08:05 to catch the 0820 train to Enfield. I was late one morning in the second week due to matters out of my control, but I knew where I was going and from then on I made my way to work alone. The Albion Road staff member, who supervised my work at the factory didn't like me anyway. This was not surprising as she was one of Peggy's friends.

After a few weeks at the factory, my supervisor accused me of doing bad work. I was convinced she had sabotaged my work in order to cause me problems. Such provocation I could not tolerate. That very day I walked out of the factory and went back to Albion Road.

In August 2005, after several telephone conversations with social services I decided to write a letter to put my case about the lack of sufficient assisted time in which to shop. The latter states:

Dear Sir/Madam

I am writing regarding time given for my shopping. I would much appreciate being given an extra half-hour as one and a half hours is not enough.

Because of my condition I need a certain number of items to see me through the week. The present limited time also makes it difficult for the person who does my shopping.

You speak of my needs not fitting your criteria. Does your criteria take mine into consideration – my changing and worsening state physically?....

You want to take away the Friday and make it another day. What difference, what help is this to me?

I would call that meaningless, mean and inconsiderate.

I'm not usually an angry person but in conversation over the phone dealing with Social Services, I find myself getting more angry and swearing at times.

*Do I have to appear on LBC radio again to put my case
if I am not dealt with satisfactorily?*
Thank You.
Miss P. Wiltshire

The Social Services is not the only public service that
is ill-prepared to deal with a disabled person. In July 2007
I had to write to British Gas after receiving a letter saying
I owed £74.00, which I knew I did not owe. When I tried
to explain on the telephone, the call centre worker was
most impolite.

In my letter I told British Gas that the person who
took my call was abrupt, impatient and should have been
better trained to deal with the public.

Even now I find it painful when I recall the barbaric
treatment meted out to me in different and diverse
situations. My mind is normal and even though I accept
my disability, I also accept myself as a person with value
and self-worth, who deserves to be treated with dignity
and respect. Charlotte was responsible for instilling in
me these positive views of myself. Society does not seem
to be able to come to terms with a black woman, who is
not physically normal, standing up for herself and having
'normal' expectations.

I know that my assessment of my situation as a disabled
person is right. If I were wrong, there would be no need
for the many demonstrations by disabled people outside
the British Parliament, the seat of 'civilised justice'.

Chapter TEN

My Disability and Illness

*D*epending on how much of my story you have read so far, you will have concluded, or I am now informing you, that I do not see myself as educationally subnormal; that my mind is intact. But it is to the severity of my disability that I now turn.

You may have exercised choice and advanced to this chapter to discover the extent of my disability. Or, you may have exercised restraint till now, to confirm what has been hinted at in the previous pages, particularly in the chapter titled Provocation. Whatever your choice, you are about to discover the extent of my multiple-physical disability.

Depending on how much of my story you have read so far, you will have concluded, or I am now informing you, that I do not see myself wearing the educationally subnormal label with ease; that my mind is intact. But it is to the severity of my disability that I now turn.

I have stated earlier that by the age of four I was aware that I was differently abled. The activities of people around me, compared with my own, told me that something was not right with me. Charlotte was gentle and sensitive in helping me to understand my situation. While helping me to do so, she also provided the psychological support for me to cope with the actuality of my differences, without allowing me to feel sorry for myself. Those lessons, if I can call them that, have and will keep me positive about myself until my dying day.

The journey to *my* realisation of my physical state was initiated by my own observations. I could not understand how Mama could put clothes on me with such ease, and I could not. Eventually I realised, it was because I was not adept with the use of one of my hands. Restrictions on playing freely, and the advanced age at which I walked, if one could call my shuffle walking, testify to a major physical defect in my leg. Then, having difficulty communicating verbally with the world around me, points to a third form of disability. These three areas of handicap qualify me to claim the multiple-disability tag. But I promised the reader details and I must be true to my word. Here are the specifics of my disability:

A baby needs two legs to balance on to make that first step. In my case, my right leg is not normal and could not support my attempts to balance and walk like most children do. With a shorter right leg, I would topple over, which forced me to the alternative of shuffling on the ground to get from place to place. As I got older, I managed to pivot on my right big toe, which gave me enough support to limp with a rise and fall motion. The pain in my right big toe was very severe, and was made worse by the weakened and undeveloped muscles in that leg from the knee downwards. Furthermore, all my toes on the right foot, apart from the big toe, are turned to the right and curved under. With such deformity in my right leg and foot, it's a blessing to have a normal big toe.

So, as far as my right leg is concerned, it was not all doom and gloom. When I was a toddler my big toe did make it possible for me to limp around and play with other children. I do recall falling to the ground frequently, but the will was there and I was not going to be beaten. The limited strength of my right leg, together with my good left leg and my *determination to succeed*, provided me with what I call my *legs of iron* – steel-like determination. I was different, but I wasn't going to let my difference get in the way of being *normal*. Painful as it was, I did walk.

If you have already read chapter seven, you will recall that my lover, Edward, helped me to wash my hair. To me that was a romantic act, which in everyday living was not absolutely necessary. I can and do wash my hair myself.

But the muscles from the elbow of my right arm to the wrist are not properly developed. Also my right hand is curved from the wrist and the fingers are not properly aligned. This makes my right arm shorter than the left. I am, therefore, unable to do some things that require dexterity, such as plaiting my hair and cutting my toenails or strenuous tasks with my upper right limb. But I can hold a glass or cup and do household chores and other work.

It is because of the physical restriction in my right arm that I had to secure the assistance of a trainee before I effectively defended myself, with my good left arm, at the Albion Road Centre, when the staff member held me by the neck (See chapter on Provocation).

The disability in my right arm makes me left-handed by default. This hasn't been a problem in itself. But where co-ordination of both hands is required, I have had to devise ways to cope – I am grateful though, that I have managed to do more than just cope with life.

My right shoulder dips lower than the left. This has had to be taken into consideration when clothes were being made for me, although with a little care in selection, I have been able to buy clothes off the peg. Compared to my leg, I don't feel that I've suffered any great disadvantage with this infirmity.

Up to now, I have only given a couple of clues from which the reader could deduce that I suffer from impaired vision. I can see people. I can see the number of the bus much better now than prior to 1997 and 2000 when I had my cataracts removed. I can read large print, but with some difficulty especially without glasses.

When I read, I hold the book about three inches away from my face. I guess that looks comical, but hey, I'm reading! As I get older, my vision has become worse and I get headaches when I read. I find it increasingly necessary to make use of the services of a carer to read my letters.

When I was a young child, my speech was nothing more than an unintelligible noise. People found it difficult to understand what I was trying to say. I knew what I wanted to communicate but couldn't form the words to give the right sounds. People didn't have the patience to listen to me or to appreciate that I needed more time to say what my brain had put together. I was often ignored or made fun of. It was frustrating and angered me, and my fuse was short. But I was not deterred; I was determined to be understood, for people to listen to me and take note.

Charlotte was my first teacher. She took the time and helped me to pronounce the letters of the alphabet. But it was Aunt Ina and the all-age school that helped me most. I was eager to go to school, just to learn to speak so I could be understood.

One teacher, Miss Ula, who had a class of forty kids, gave me the time and attention I needed. She didn't have to, for it was an ordinary class I was in, in an ordinary school. During breaks, Miss Ula would sit me down and took me painstakingly through the pronunciation of words. I worked hard and whenever I called out a word relatively clearly, I could see the smile of satisfaction on her face. That was a source of encouragement in itself.

Miss Ula's selfless dedication, and that of others before her and since, has paid off. My speech, presently, is not what the Queen of England would call normal, but if I got the chance, I could hold a conversation with her or anyone else, without comprehension being lost.

By society's norm, I'm an ill person. I am officially diagnosed with cerebral palsy, thus the symptoms I've outlined above. Between the ages of ten and fifteen I suffered from fits, yet I have never been to a doctor for treatment, nor have I taken any medication for it. Luckily, I have never been in any dangerous situation when I had seizures. There was always someone nearby to protect me from hurting myself. I have not had any repeats of those seizures since I was fifteen.

My main recurring illness has been colds. I also developed asthma in 1989, which is still with me and which I treat with the usual inhaler. When I get colds together with asthma, I become absolutely miserable which I try to contain and just keep wishing the ailment away.

Even though I am regarded as not being fit and healthy, prior to 2006 and excluding the four and a half years I spent in the special hospital in Kingston, Jamaica, I had only been kept in hospital twice. The first time was when I just arrived in England: they thought that because I was very skinny something was wrong with me, so I was admitted and kept in hospital under observation for a week. In 1984 I had a hysterectomy. This was because my monthly became bi-monthly and was very heavy. I spent one week in hospital and another convalescing.

In 1987 I did a lot of walking and standing while visiting Jamaica. On my way back, I had to stand for a long time at Gatwick airport, while waiting for wheelchair assistance, and afterwards for my lift to take me home. After waiting in vain for my lift, I took a taxi home and learnt later that the car that was to collect me had broken down on its way to the airport.

When I got to my flat, very tired and thirsty, I made my way to the kitchen to make a cup of tea. I reached to my right to pick up a cup, and by doing so transferred most of my weight to my right leg. There was a sudden 'pop', signalling that something had broken. I eased the weight off my right foot and had to hop to a chair. Just then my son and my friend arrived. They helped me into bed, where I waited until the morning to call the doctor.

I telephoned the surgery as soon as it opened and requested a visit, carefully explaining my situation. The doctor stupidly told me to come in to the surgery. I explained that if I *could* come to the surgery, I wouldn't be asking for a visit. When the doctor arrived, he declared that I had broken my ankle. I told him that it was my instep. But, insistently, he gave me a note to have my ankle X-rayed. At the hospital they wouldn't listen to me either. The pain was excruciating. I went home in tears, called another doctor from my GP's practice, who said, "It isn't normal for Pauline to be crying." I was taken to the hospital again where this time they set my instep and put it in plaster of Paris, which stayed on for six weeks.

I was astonished when the doctor, who said it was my ankle that was broken, sent me a note encouraging me to find another GP Practice. I telephoned him immediately and said, "You are my doctor but I am the patient. I am no fool. I am not looking for no (sic) other doctor." I was told after that incident, that he was known to pick and choose his patients.

Once the fracture had healed, I was measured up for callipers to support my instep. This was fitted to my right shoe and extended to just below my knee. At first the callipers felt heavy, they still do, but it was the slight embarrassment I felt when wearing them that I had to deal with. I told myself that it was better to have the callipers and be able to walk 'normally' than not to walk at all. The freedom of walking far outweighed the embarrassment of using callipers.

Fitting the callipers, which I believe is a good device, did affect my way of walking. The built-up sole of the right shoe eliminated the rising and falling motion that I had been accustomed to all my life up to 1992, as my right leg is shorter than the left. Apart from the little added weight, the only disadvantage is that I have to have all my shoes specially made. However, I tell myself that handmade shoes are to be preferred to those mass made by machine. What is more I have the assurance that my instep will not breakdown again, so I step out with confidence.

Clearly, the strength of the iron support, which wasn't necessary before I broke my instep, has served me well. Leg of iron? Yes. But it did not replace my figurative *legs of iron*, that strong mental will and determination that Charlotte helped to instil in me from birth, which I have used to carry me through life's maze of troubles and trials as well as its joys and celebrations. But as a disabled black woman, I knew I would still have to face whatever society threw at me. And for that reason, I knew I would always need my original and invisible *legs of iron* to keep me positive, to keep me going, buoyant and victorious.

Presently (2007), I have arthritis in my back and my good left leg. Severe pain in my left hip makes me reliant on a walking stick for support, particularly when I go out. Otherwise I get around fairly well, even with a few extra pounds in weight gained since I came to England.

For many years I have had help with my shopping. My hand and back hurt so I do appreciate the help. Since 2000 I've had a regular home-help service. This has proven invaluable in helping me to live a normal life.

Pain isn't nice and I get my fair share. But I know that all of us, normal or disabled, do get a cocktail of pain as we get older. All of us are destined to die. Even doctors die. My aim is to be normal in my thinking, while seeking to maintain a decent quality of life for as long as I am able to. And even though my illness gets me down at times, I know that that is normal for all of us.

I look forward to going to heaven when Jesus comes. There will be no more pain, no abnormality, no more injustice, no more sorrow or death. This is the hope I live by now. Until then, I go on living and hoping for better times, while accepting the realities of life.

Chapter ELEVEN

My World of Work

*E*ventually, *I told my boss that I couldn't continue to work for such a low wage, as my needs were more than £10 a week could meet.*

There is a text in the Bible, which says, "If a man will not work, he shall not eat." (2 Thessalonians 3: 10). I don't wish to take an overly simplistic view of this text, but it's obvious that if no one worked, there would be no food for anyone.

Some of the most important jobs are done in the home, caring for the family. In most westernised societies more and more people are being employed to do housework. In the developing countries where there is a stark difference between rich and poor, the maid employment industry is well established. The work that is paid for in that industry occurs in every household, the majority as chores without direct remuneration. Such essential duties in ordinary households should not be underestimated just because the people who do them do not often get paid.

From my earliest years, I have been occupied around the home doing chores that could be seen to be well above my years and ability. I cared for children, cleaned houses, swept yards, cooked meals on open wood fires, washed clothes by hand and what have you, both before and after my first paid job.

The library in Christiana, Manchester, Jamaica, provided me with my first earned income. I was a general hand at the library, stamping books, sorting newspapers, cleaning, and the rest. There were just the two of us and Laurel treated me very well. My pay was five shillings (25p) per week and I stayed there for five years, until I was 19 years old.

Aunt Ina's husband had a lumber business. He would stockpile the freshly sawn or acquired lumber in the yard. There was always a pile waiting for collection or stock awaiting someone to purchase it. There was no one at home during the day – Aunt Ina was at school, I was at the library and her husband was out preparing new lumber for his business.

I found out that people would help themselves to lumber from the yard without paying for it. One evening, Aunt Ina's husband was furious. He said a lot of his prized timber had been stolen and he was particularly uneasy because a merchant was due to collect his order the next day. The thief had left only half of what had been stockpiled to meet the order. There was nothing he could do to make up the order in such a short time and he wasn't the kind of person to give an excuse or not to keep his word to his clients. He decided to act to prevent his stock being stolen again. Who would stay home to guard the lumber? It couldn't be Aunt Ina and certainly not her husband. Would it be the weakest link? Me, or somebody else?

"Pauline" he called. "From next week you have to stay home and watch the lumber."

That was it. No discussion.

At least I had almost a week to give in my notice at the library. Laurel was very understanding when I explained the situation and my leaving so suddenly. She thanked me for working with her and for being so industrious.

The next Monday morning I started my new unpaid job as a lumberyard watchman. I stood on the steps of Aunt Ina's house and stared at the heaps of lumber. Some freshly cut, others dark brown showing weather worn signs. One lot displayed blackened toadstools, a testimony that they have remained undisturbed for years – a couple of goats sat comfortably resting on it. There were other piles just wearing their characteristic colours, but all motionless, sleeping horizontally in their own beds.

I wanted to curse the thieves that came and disturbed the sleeping lumber and carried it away by day, when no one was around to speak-up for the neuter gender. Now, I was given that job. I would have to prevent anyone taking the lumber. I was its protector.

I wasn't paid for my new 'job', but neither did I pay anything towards my full board at Aunt Ina's. So, in a way, I was now paying in kind. But I missed receiving my five shillings a week from the library.

In addition to watching the lumber, (Actually I didn't actively watch anything. It was just my presence at home and the fact that I had a mouth to report back, which was the deterrent), I had to do the family laundry most days. Yes, there were maids, but none of them stayed long, so inevitably there was laundry for me to do.

Mothers in the vicinity became aware that I was at home and brought there children for me to look after while they went on errands, attended to their animals, worked their fields or whatever they did. This work was a labour of love. There was a community expectation that anyone who was available would help those in need. Occasionally I would get a few shillings from Aunt Ina or her husband. David's father couldn't help me. He needed help himself.

It was in England, seven years after leaving Laurel and the library, that I got my next regular income. At the Albion Road Centre I counted batches of 12 plastic bags for someone else to seal in another bag. I was paid £4 a week for this work, but I soon got the hang of it and after two weeks I was promoted to 'sealing' only.

Charlotte was long dead, but her words kept echoing in my head: "Pauline, pray to God and He will help you to look after yourself." I was in England, the mother country, and I was convinced that if I prayed to God for sustenance and worked hard, God was going to help me to help myself. I did my best at sealing the batches of twelve plastic bags in one and packing them away. Soon, several trainees were feeding me with batches of twelve. My efforts were rewarded and I earned bonuses, bringing my weekly earnings up to £14 at times.

The Albion Road Centre job was not just work for earning money. The clients were called trainees, and rightly so, for training was part of the reason for the centre's existence. I decided to learn embroidery. It was difficult at first but I soon got the hang of it and enjoyed my new found skill.

When I left Albion Road Centre the first time, I went to a factory where I did a similar type of work, packing things in boxes. The bags, however, were counted by machines. I would either feed the machine with bags or take away the collated batches and stock or box them.

The factory wasn't a comfortable place. There was no seat and the long time spent standing was very uncomfortable for me. It was cold, the people were unfriendly and my line manager was always on my back. In addition, the train rides to the factory were horrible; the trains were packed like sardines and standing for the journey was most distressing. The days were very hard. To add insult to injury, I was paid much less than when I was at Albion Road.

On one of my half days off work, by this point I was back working at Albion Road, my mum sent me to a local health food store, to buy some groceries. The manager, who was at the till, engaged me in conversation. As I paid for the groceries and was about to leave he asked, "By the way, are you looking for work?" Without hesitation I said, "Yes."

My stay at the Albion Road Centre didn't last long the second time round. The hours at my new job weren't fixed. Sometimes I worked a few hours a day and occasionally I'd do a 10 to 2 shift. I was paid £1.50 per hour for doing a variety of tasks. In a reference the manager wrote for me some time later he said, "Some of her duties included packing, serving customers, cleaning and childcare. She is punctual, clean, neat and straightforward."

I also went to my new boss's home and did the family's laundry. The pay was never more than £10 per week. In addition I worked for his wife cleaning a school for four hours a week for no additional pay. Eventually, I told my boss that I couldn't continue to work for such a low wage, as my needs were more than £10 a week could meet.

Further hunting secured me a job cleaning a private home for a family with a newly born baby. I was given lunch each day, paid well, but sadly the work was only for a year. Other jobs, mostly part-time, included six months for Hackney Council at County Hall working with a small group that selected the stories to be included in their disability newspaper; thirteen years at Sunrise School as an assistant, and a spell at Sunshine Nursery demonstrating to teenagers how to put nappies on babies.

On one occasion, while working at the County Hall editorial assistant job, our line manager decided that our work wasn't good enough so we wouldn't be paid. I happened to know that she was the wife of Mr Bernie Grant MP. I was elected to approach her to discuss the matter. The line manager wasn't in when I phoned her office but I told the secretary to tell her that I happened to know that her husband was a black man and if she did not pay us, I would go directly to him. The problem was resolved without further discussion. We all got paid. Each member of the group was so delighted with the outcome that they contributed to a generous sum, which they gave me. The presenter said, "If it wasn't for you Pauline, we wouldn't have gotten anything."

After a period of unemployment, the wife of my boss from the health store asked me to clean the school again, but this time at a better hourly rate. I was expected to clean the whole primary school, alone, in two hours. This was impossible. I didn't stay long in that job as it was stressing me out. Too much was expected of me in too little time.

About this time I had my first attempt at writing a book, *Now I Live in England*. I went up and down, as it were, trying to sell my photocopied book to anyone who would buy it, at 30p a copy. Unsurprisingly not many copies were sold as it was poorly presented.

From then on I did small jobs in peoples' homes, but eventually and inevitably, my main income was from Social Security as ill health had taken its effect on me.

****

At home, and over the years, since Jamaica, I have developed my culinary skills. I am an above average cook and I often entertain people from church. I give parties, for which I prepare the dishes, and also bake cakes. My favourite dish is Rice and Peas (red beans or gungo peas) with stewed Chicken, Jamaican style. But I can also do a variety of *wicked* vegetarian dishes. My special drink is my own concocted flavoured carrot juice and a popular dessert is my flavoured custard with a piece of my cake.

For my parties I would provide a variety of dishes, which could include:

- Plain rice and/or rice 'n' peas
- Roasted potatoes (ordinary and/or sweet)
- Pasta (plain) and/or macaroni 'n' cheese

The main protein choice would be:
- Fried and/or stewed fish
- Roasted and/or stewed chicken

- Roasted mutton (in the oven)
- Salt-fish 'n' Ackee (a Jamaican specialty)

Sometimes the people I entertained are vegetarians. I would then substitute meat dishes with Quorn, mock duck and/or vege-mince. These would be cooked up with thyme, onions, black pepper, garlic, tomato, etc to give a flavour that is satisfying to the taste buds.

Afters could include:
- Plain and/or fruit and coconut cakes and vanilla or rum 'n' raisin ice cream

Drinks would not be alcoholic. So a variety of:
- Fruit juices, home-made carrot juice (spiced up with a dash of cinnamon, nutmeg, vanilla, etc)

One side-item that is always a favourite, and which goes well with ackee 'n' salt-fish, chicken, fish and other proteins, is buttered hard-dough bread. This is readily available in many local shops that carry Caribbean goods. At a push, it could be substituted with any white bread – preferably un-sliced.

Depending on the size of the gathering, I would get help, which is readily available, but I would often plan the menu.

***

I believe I have special green fingers. My houseplants and potted plants outside are lush and their healthy state gives me the satisfaction that I'm doing something else that's good. I still have a flower garden, which I tend myself with much joy. For many years I had a much bigger flower garden outside, which I also tended myself. Sadly, because of problems with my back, I have had to pave over most of it. But the reduced size only gives me more time to focus on other things, such as the conceiving of this book, which is just another form of work that the next chapter will explain.

Chapter TWELVE

My Education and Writing

While I have not been to any of the academically recognised tertiary educational institutions, I have spent most of my time at the university-of-life. There the teachers give you no formal feedback. The lessons are often harsh and experiential and only the wise learn quickly.

Education? Am I being presumptuous in referring to myself as having an education? Whilst specialist educators may define education to mean something other than what I have acquired, I'm quite comfortable using the following four definitions, with added emphases, from the Yahoo Internet Dictionary to describe my education:

- The *act or process* of educating or being educated.
- The *knowledge or skill* obtained or developed by a learning process.
- A *program of instruction* of a specified kind or level

- An *instructive or enlightening experience*

My earliest recollection of formally engaging in *the act or process of being educated* was when I was five years old in hospital in Kingston, Jamaica. I learned to write my name and read. But even though my mind recalls the hospital's instruction and the learning process, I know that my first teacher was in fact Charlotte.

Charlotte taught me how to read, write, and count before I went to the hospital. I probably shouldn't count that as schooling as that was more what a mama does for her daughter. I didn't make much progress, but the exercise was fun and gave the basis for the formal process at the hospital's school to build on.

To me, the experience of Charlotte's home teaching was normal, but others looking on might not have thought so. It was normal because Charlotte was imparting knowledge to me that was relevant to my life. She was very patient and did not treat me or allow me to feel that I was abnormally different.

The *process* of learning, both for reading and writing, had to involve the book being held close to my face, inches away. After leaving hospital, and as I got older, even while going to teenage school, reading materials still had to be held close to my eyes. Fine print, particularly the Bible, was challenging. But I was determined to read and write like anybody else, so how I looked during the *act* of acquiring those skills didn't matter to me. I regarded myself as a slow learner when compared to others my age. But somehow I never link this slowness of learning with my impaired sight.

Up to the time of leaving Jamaica to England at the age of 26, I had had no glasses to correct my poor vision. Within a year of coming to England I got a set, which helped me to see a little better, but not significantly more, as my retinas were damaged. I now realise that as I get older, I find it more difficult to spell and my sight seems to be deteriorating, but I am still reading, even with the book hugging my face.

The knowledge or skill obtained or developed by a learning process at the Albion Road Centre, including embroidery, whetted my appetite to engage in more formal learning. So at age 28, I started evening classes at the William Paten School in Stoke Newington. It was a normal adult evening class, not one for the disabled. There I did more reading, writing and a little one-handed typing.

While I was at William Patten, I had the idea of writing my story. It was after the teacher asked us to write something about ourselves that I decided to, and wrote a short piece about my life. The teacher read my work to the class and everyone agreed that it was very good. That encouragement was the new beginning for me to *develop* a new *skill* – writing.

With the *program of instruction of a specified kind*, creative writing, my education travelled along a new direction. I told myself, 'If I can write a short story which people enjoyed, why can't I write a book?' For the next weeks, after the teacher read out my piece, I used class time to embark on the challenging road of writing.

I transferred to Centerprise Trust and did more focused writing lessons, which helped me to complete the first draft of my first 'book' and start another. After Centerprise, I attended day classes at Brook House Boys

School (now Hackney College), where I developed my reading and writing skills further. During this time I became ill and I was provided with a Home Tutor, who, and with a lot of patience on both sides, helped me to put the finishing touches to my 'book', *Now I Live in England*. The three years the Home Tutor spent with me were nevertheless most useful. My dream of seeing my story appearing in print was being realised. I knew in my mind that this was just the beginning and I dreamt of bigger things, even though I also knew that I had to depend on others to help me to fulfil those dreams.

***

Now I Live in England didn't do well. It wasn't well presented and looked more like a few sheets of paper clipped together. However, Centerprise took more interest in my writing and I combined the material from *Now I Live in England* with new material to produce what I call my second book, *Living and Winning*, which did very well, selling almost four thousand copies. A new day was dawning for me. Investment in my education was paying dividends. My story caught the imagination of the media and I received invitations and appeared in schools, colleges, a university and even on Channel 4 television.

Looking back, there were of course many more difficulties involved in producing *Living and Winning*, largely because those who were helping me, were mostly white or black people who behaved as if they were white, all with good intentions. They didn't understand my culture or background or didn't want to know, or they were too inpatient to take the time to find out what I was trying to achieve when I couldn't find the words to express myself clearly.

Even though *Living and Winning* was relatively successful for me, reviewers, Jan Mckenley and Suzanne Scafe, expressed some of what it lacked. They wrote:

"The style is a mixture of anecdote and understatement which, though often unexpected, is very effective... But there are also moments when one would have wished for greater elaboration of her feelings and a clearer insight into her more troubled moments and difficult relationships...

"The least appealing aspect of the book is its packaging... a throwback to a '70s' experience when the 'powerless' were grateful for the patronage of the white social/community workers. In 1985 the relationship ought to be more equal than this format suggests."

Even with the above reservations on the quality of *Living and Winning,* playwright Philomena Sykie captured the story in a play, *The Cripple,* which was performed at several venues throughout England. It was well received and had a number of healthy reviews.

***

I have applied three of the four definitions of education given at the beginning of this chapter. The fourth, *An instructive or enlightening experience,* forms the larger part of my education.

While I have not been to any of the academically recognised tertiary educational institutions, I have spent most of my time at the *university-of-life.* There the teachers give you no formal feedback. The lessons are often harsh and experiential and only the wise learn quickly.

I have attended the university-of-life since I was with Charlotte in Jamaica. The same university is in England too, where I have attended for longer. I am still in attendance and will continue to my dying day. How much I have learned is for you to determine. I have no diplomas or certificates to prove my attendance – my university does not deal with paper or technology. It has no physical presence - but in it I have been *enlightened* through the *instructive* lessons of hard knocks, mental scars, and injustice thrown at me.

I have experienced dual racism, as a black woman and a disabled person, and have many times been treated as less than human. I have been exploited and abused, but I have had some good times, contributed positively to society, far above that which a multiple-physically disabled person is expected to. On the other hand, I have been appreciated, loved, valued and listened to, too. At the end of the day I can testify that I have walked the corridors of the university-of-life. I have lived through it all.

Through living, I have come to accept reality, my reality. I have accepted my own limitations. I have often prayed to God, as Charlotte taught me to do, to send me a British person with a genuine Jamaican background to help me, so I could produce a better book to reflect more truly my experience, which I hope the public could benefit from, and therefore learn to appreciate disabled people more. This book in your hand, I believe, is the answer to my prayers.

Chapter THIRTEEN

Planning Ahead

I have consulted with the ministers whom I hope will officiate at my funeral service and one has assisted me in selecting the grave spot.

I'm aware that planning ahead is a key requirement for successful living. Planning ahead is the right of every human being who is able to do so, and while I do not particularly want every detail of my life to be charted, I believe that some important aspects should not be left to chance.

Diana, Princess of Wales, had a detailed will while she was still very young, because she wanted to protect her sons. This encouraged me to sort out that aspect of my life while I'm still able to, and before it is too late. In a sense, I've decided not only to make a will, so that the insignificant amount of this world's goods that I possess – mostly my personal effects – go to where I would like them to end up, but also to plan my funeral almost in its entirety, leaving very little planning or headaches for those who will administer that event. Of course I'll not be able to have the programme printed ahead of time, as things like the date of my death won't be known to me.

Is it bizarre for me to be so particular about events following my death? I don't think so. That's why I've decided to put things and people in charge of what will happen to me after I die.

As well as the good example of Diana, and I'm sure many more ordinary and not-so-ordinary people, who have done likewise, I'm partly guided by the principle of a text in the Bible which says, "A man might have a hundred children and live a long time, but what good is it if he can't enjoy the good God gives him or have a proper burial? (Ecclesiastes 6: 3, New Century Version).

But of more importance is the treatment I've experienced, as a disabled person: people talking about me as if I'm not there, sometimes depriving me of basic human needs, my close family not looking out for me and so on. These things have forced me to make arrangements for my funeral and leave the execution of my plans in the hands of those I know will do the right thing on my behalf.

What arrangements have I made so far? I have consulted with the ministers whom I hope to officiate at my funeral service and one has assisted me in selecting the grave spot, casket (cream colour), dress (also cream), undertakers (Caribbean style), the headstone with wording (being finalised) are in place, and I've also decided on a lawn type grave for easy aftercare. I've selected hymns and readings, and four photos depicting different phases of my life, to be included on the programme.

I have no photos of my childhood so the earliest, other than my passport photo, is of when I first came to England. The other three represent aspects of my life up to the present. There are some things I have decided to leave to the discretion of my church and family. These are to include tributes and refreshments at the reception after the burial. All the other major items listed above are being paid for on a monthly basis and hopefully the proceeds from this book will help.

My planning ahead for events that will take place after I have died, is to fulfill the desire for things to be done decently and in order then. I can now, therefore, put the final events that will take place immediately after my life on earth has ended, out of my active thoughts. I am confident that when I go there won't be too much pressure on my family, so I'm now free to focus on living whilst enjoying the gifts of life and the beauty of planet earth, which I intend to see more of in my travels.

Chapter FOURTEEN

My Travels

I have come to realise that the best and most economical way to facilitate travelling to different places is to make friends with people of different nationalities where you live and work.

This chapter is not intended to be a travelogue, but rather to reflect my interest as a disabled person in travelling and seeing new places.

Generally, I don't talk about my life to people I come in contact with on a daily basis. Moreover, these days I don't get to go out much as my back and my good leg hurt a lot. I get quite lonely at times sitting at home, but my mind is out there, wanting to explore the nooks and crannies of God's fascinating earth and man's own creations, which are concentrated in cities and across waterways. Television brings some wonderful and fascinating nature programmes into my living room, and the world of sports and exploration are only a click of a remote control button away. But I often get the urge to go and see or experience the events and soak up the atmosphere for myself.

When I was in Jamaica I didn't travel much, but I guess my early trips to Kingston, the capital of Jamaica, for medical reasons might have instilled the bug of travelling into my interestingly shaped bones and mind. I suspect my mind didn't associate the experience of travelling to and from Kingston to disability. Rather, I was seeing new things, enjoying the rides and the excitement of eating in new places away from home and getting pleasure from it. All this added to the quest for exploration.

I have come to realise that the best and most economical way to facilitate travelling to different places is to make friends with people of different nationalities where you live and work. In addition, Social Services saw it as their pleasant duty to take us unfortunate disabled souls, on holiday. Those trips were always welcomed. I enjoyed those weeks away for as long as they lasted. In time they were stopped due to cutbacks. Maybe that is why I have, subsequent to cut backs, ventured further a field at my own expense. A change of routine, of scenery, of eating rooms, of menus, and even of the chair one sits on creates new ambience, new thoughts and feelings. Even just to walk down an unfamiliar street gives me a buzz of newness, of exploration. So it is not necessarily the distance I travel that gives that special buzz, the holiday feeling, but the change of environment. There is always something special that's attached to taking an aeroplane or a cruise ship and handing over my passport for checking.

Jamaica, my first home, is special. I love going back. So far I have been back to Jamaica five times. The first time was in 1982 when I spent three months catching up with my son, David. I returned in 1986 for one month and in 1992 for another month, spending quality time with Aunt Ina who was quite ill. She died soon after I returned. Then in 1999, I spent just two weeks there with another month in 2004. I paid for all those visits myself, except for the 1986 trip which was paid for from the proceeds of the play, *The Cripple,* which was based on my book *Living and Winning.* Other travels took me to Sweden for a week in 1982 before I went to Jamaica that year. It was a cruise with a group organised by a local Anglican church.

As I have said, friendship is a good way to facilitate travelling. In 1993 I visited Canada for a month and stayed with a friend. Other travels to see friends include a week in France; a month with a friend in St. Vincent (I used to look after his grandchild in London); nine weeks in Dominica. I have travelled to many places around the British Isles for weekends and longer visits, and twice to Belgium, once for a week.

I have been to America to see my mother three times and I am due to go again, this time to see my adopted father too. I don't know what the average travel is for a normal person in Britain, but I am delighted that I have had the opportunity to travel, to discover new places and feed my mind on new sights. How much more I travel in the future will depend largely on the success of my book and my health. I guess this is a normal expectation. I am not denying the fact that my disability does impact the ease and the extent to which I can enjoy my travels. But I accept my disability, realising that the different conditions do cause limitations. I focus on what I can enjoy when I am out there, not on what I cannot.

One of the many benefits of having travelled is the experience gained from observing the sights, customs, people and their habits in the various countries I've visited. The value of such experience cannot be over emphasised, particularly in the case of a disabled person, who, with life's restraints and in my case, inability to drive, has to spend more time at home than I would like. I would have liked to have the freedom that being able to drive brings. But since driving did not present itself to me as an option, I just never thought of it as a hurdle I should seek to conquer.

When I travel now, I feel I have to observe and take in more of the sights than my able-bodied counterparts do. I feel I need the extra information, more mental pictures to call on for my 'mind-entertainment,' whenever I'm alone and want to watch a mental movie as I reflect on my past encounters. This ability to vividly recall the scenery and joyous experiences I've had in the various countries I have visited is very comforting to me.

Of the countries I have travelled, excluding Jamaica, my first home, I find Toronto in Canada to be the most appealing. I simply describe it as 'nice'. It is very attractive and clean. Even the tramps on the streets seem to be of a higher calibre than in any of the other countries I have travelled, including England. There was an absence of street violence or even rowdiness, and the people seem to go about their business in a quiet and purposeful manner.

My presence did not draw any marked attention; at least they did not stop and stare at me as if I'm one of those green people from Mars. The streets were free of disabled people. This, though, may be due to the fact that they moved about in private cars. There seemed to be very little public transport. If the impression I had of public transport in Canada was the case in London, I would not be able to get around as much as I do now, which would greatly impair my freedom. I was very surprised to see the huge shopping malls. Their vastness, variety and quantity made me feel I was watching a movie on a giant screen. I loved it.

In the West Indies, I found Dominicans quite similar in friendliness to Jamaicans. But there was this other streak to the Dominicans: In public places they would stare at me as if they had never seen a disabled person before. I imagined that they must have locked theirs away in their homes and were thinking that I may have escaped. Like Sweden, I did not see any disabled people in wheelchairs in Dominica. Another thing about the Dominicans, was that they would speak slowly to me, drawing out each word and emphasising each syllable in their interesting accent, as if they were on a mission to ensure I could understand them. I found their efforts very interesting and gave them my attention with a fixed smile.

The Dominicans, though, were very helpful: Whenever a set of steps presented itself to be scaled, there would inevitably be a remark or two, or a quick movement in my direction from someone nearby. They would insist on helping me up the stairs, to which I would simply say, "No thank you. I'm fine." Often I would be told before entering a church, "You cannot go up those steps."

"How do you know if I can go up the steps or not?" I would not wait for an answer – there would be none - and I would just continue walking, aided by my stick as the little crowd watch me ascend. On one occasion I did not have my stick and a lady offered her assistance to help me climbed the steps. I did not hesitate to recognise my need and said, "Yes, thank you."

I'm planning on doing more travelling. Antigua and Barbados are the next two new countries I would like to visit. I have friends from these countries that go on holiday regularly. It is highly likely, though, that I'll revisit Jamaica and Florida, before I venture on other expeditions, as I'm due to go and see some 'long time friends' and my aging mother. But whether I visit a new country or one that I've already visited, I would like this book to be published first, so I can take some with me.

It is my strong belief that society should come to realise that the disabled are human beings, with ability, potential, needs, feelings and zest to live life to its fullness. I believe every one of us has some disability – marked or not. The focus of my life therefore is to do what I can, how I can and when I can. So please excuse me if I can't see myself the way you see me. I have decided to pull along this disabled body of mine to do and achieve what it can.

Join me or just watch me go on my *legs of iron*.